In Praise for

"It's ironic. We know better than to walk into a department store and pick out the ugliest outfit. Or to scan a menu and order the dish we least desire. But in our thinking, we often pick out thoughts that do not serve us, thoughts that actually hurt us. Especially when it comes to death. This paradigm-shifting book offers us "fresh thoughts, fresh beliefs" about the most feared event of our lives and the lives of our loved ones. Anna Enea gives us a blueprint for waking up, for discovering life beyond the physical and for staying eternally connected to those on the other side of the veil."

—PAM GROUT, #1 NEW YORK TIMES BESTSELLING AUTHOR OF
E-SQUARED, THE COURSE IN MIRACLES EXPERIMENT AND 18
OTHER BOOKS

Anna tells the story of her painful, outer journey that turned into inner work. She performed alchemy that turned a tragedy into a spiritual awakening. This book is a guiding light for the journey through the most painful, traumatic experiences in life. She found freedom through devastating experiences that cause most people to fall apart. She used meditation as self-discovery and salvation back to the Source within. She has truly tapped into the unconditional love beyond the manifest, physical world. I highly recommend this book to anyone who has suffered from the loss of a loved one.

—GURUDEV SHRI AMRITJI DESAI

Together Forever is brave and powerful and provides a clear roadmap to a realm unconceived in modern language and thinking. Anna Marie teaches us how to transform tragedy into abundance, gratitude, and Divine love. Through the practice of acceptance and presence, she has laid the foundation for us to walk a true bridge to the Divine. *Together Forever* is a most important and life changing read.

My friendship with Anna Marie began in catholic high school. Anna Marie was inspirational for me then and more recently she catalyzed one of the most powerful changes in my life. Over the years, my spiritual side had taken a back seat to my finance career. To rebalance my life, I attended several of Anna Marie's yoga and meditation retreats in San Gemini, Italy. A life-altering experience happened to me during one of our meditation sessions and at that moment I became a true believer in the Truth of Anna Marie's teachings. My mother had died a few months before the retreat and during this meditation session, I clearly saw my mother's face and she was trying to reach me, attempting to push through a plastic-like veil. She could not pierce the veil, but I knew it was my mom and that she was guiding me to follow this path. This was my awakening to the transformative power of meditation and the reality of divine connection, and I have maintained a deep meditation and spiritual practice since.

—*MELINDA EISENHUT DUNN, RETIRED CHIEF FINANCIAL/ COMPLIANCE OFFICER, BOARD MEMBER*

Osho once said that loneliness is missing a loved one and aloneness is being your higher Self. When you are one with your higher Self, you are communing with everyone in the universe especially with your loved ones. Anna calls it vibrational relationships. "Together Forever" takes us on a journey from loss to acceptance to awakening to our true authentic Self, in a heartwarming story. This book is full of practical gems, which will bring one to living their best possible life in body, mind, and spirit. This book is very timely, especially in these changing times when so many have lost so much.

—*VIJAY K. JAIN M.D. PRESIDENT AND FOUNDER OF INTERNATIONAL UNIVERSITY OF YOGA AND AYURVEDA*

Together Forever

Using Adversity For Awakening
Illuminating The Bridge From Earth To Heaven

Anna Marie Enea

Dedication

This book is dedicated to my sons, Sal and Arthur, who bless and inspire me daily with their humor, support, kindness, and unconditional love— Sal from the formless realm and Arthur, here on earth.

This book is written in honor of my loving mother, Elizabeth Macaluso Enea, and others like her who have suffered deeply from loss.

CONTENTS

PART II: Connection and Signs

Part III: Transcendence

INTRODUCTION

Goodbyes are only for those who love with their eyes. Because for those who love with heart and soul there is no such thing as separation.

–RUMI, THIRTEENTH-CENTURY SCHOLAR AND POET

It is my hope that if you have experienced a deep loss *Together Forever* will lead you on a journey to explore, expand, and experience your infinite potential. This book is for everyone, because at some point in our lives, if we live long enough, we all experience loss—loss of someone we cherish, adore, and love beyond what words can describe or loss of health, home, job, security, and so forth. All forms of loss have the potential for self-destruction, as well as opportunities for growth, woven into the fabric of the trauma.

This book is an exploration of life, love, and of an *awakening* to our *true essence*. It is written to awaken you to a new way of viewing what our culture calls *death* and what I call *transition*. It will help you recognize that death is the opposite of birth not the opposite of life. Life always continues for us, it just changes form. This book will introduce a new paradigm of how we can respond to loss with grace and growth, instead of pain and endless suffering. And in our response we will be led by our hearts, in coherence with our minds, to a deep and lasting journey of Self-Realization.

This is *not* another book on grief and how to survive loss. Rather this book speaks of love, of the deepest love. This love is real and goes beyond this physical world. There is no end to this love. Nothing can ever threaten this love. This love has no opposite, because it is based in the eternal essence of your being. If you are reading this book, it is my guess that you have this deep love connection with someone and maybe with several others. This kind of love is free, priceless, and can never be threatened.

I lost my son, Sal, when he was twenty-four, in a motorcycle accident. I wrote this book for those of us who have lost a love so all-encompassing that it feels like this loss might actually kill you or destroy the life you have left.

My sincere intention in writing this book is to offer you another way. As you travel the pages of this book, my hope is you come to know that in reality there is no death, no separation. You will realize, that through the loss of a loved one, your own heart and mind have the capacity to expand and be open to new possibilities that you never knew existed.

Every time one person chooses a new way to respond to the challenges of life, each time an individual chooses a new option, that person then becomes a living bridge for all the others who choose to follow in that person's path.

–Gregg Braden, Scientist, Author, Lecturer

We do not have many examples of how to respond to life's tragedies in a way that is empowering to our own well-being. In fact, in some cultures, we are expected to be depressed and in a dark place after losing a child, a spouse, or a very close loved one. In many places in the world, women are required to wear black for the rest of their lives after losing a spouse or a child. I'll never forget, when I was twenty-two years old, backpacking through Europe and spending time on the island of Corfu in Greece, I saw many women dressed in all black clothing everyday. These women appeared tired and unhappy. I later learned the custom of widows on Corfu, they are expected by society to wear black after the loss of a husband or child, on this incredibly beautiful island with the most brilliant sunsets. What a paradox! This is an outdated tradition and can curtail ones opportunity for growth.

I would like to offer another way, a positive way of dealing with the loss. The truth that revealed itself on my journey through loss is this: *there is an opportunity in every heartbreak, challenge, and loss, for a life filled with a deeper inner peace, grace, gratitude, joy, and love than ever before.* As you read this book, you will discover the undeniably miracles that show up when you have the courage to accept the unacceptable.

Throughout this book I will refer to death as a transition. Because that is exactly what it is, a transition of energy—the way water can be solid ice, liquid, or vapor. Our true essence is invisible and formless, the body is our physical form. When we die our consciousness is not in that familiar body anymore; however, it is still present. It can be sensed and perceived by our awareness, but it cannot be seen by our eyes. So yes there is death of the physical body, but not of the consciousness of your loved one.

I do not claim to know the details of what happens after we leave our physical body. I know that love knows no death. I know for sure we are all connected and one with our Source. I know this because of my own direct experiences, which I will share in this book.

We are not these bodies; we're neither our accomplishments nor our possessions—we are all one with the Source of all being, which is God.

–Anita Moorjani, Author, Teacher

My response to my son's death was different than anything that I had witnessed before. The one thing in life that we as human beings have, that no one can take from us, is our response to what happens in life.

This is not to say that I was not devastated from Sal's unexpected death. I was completely devastated, I was in shock, and I felt a huge void in my heart and life. Of course, I still miss the physical Sal, and I would never say it was a gift to lose my son. But, I did not lose Sal, he is with me more than ever, but in a very different way, which will be described throughout this book. As you read, it may sound that it was easy for me and that I did not feel pain. No, for me, losing a child was the greatest challenge in all of my life. What I had always considered the worst thing that could happen to me, did happen. And after all of this, my life is filled with deeper peace, love, and joy.

Long ago, I chose a lifestyle and work that would promote health and peace in my life as well as spiritual growth, I valued these more than anything else and I had a strong desire to help others. My work for the past thirty-seven years has been and continues to be in teaching meditation, yoga, health and wellness, and spirituality.

When I lost Sal, I turned to the spiritual and practical principles that I knew so well. As it turned out, following my heart and keeping my daily morning practice of meditation, yoga, expressing gratitude, and walking in nature created by default another way of dealing with grief and loss.

One of my favorite topics to teach in my classes is how science and spirituality have come together in recent years. I have attended many workshops to study with revolutionary scientists who specialize in the field, including Gregg Braden, Bruce Lipton, and Joe Dispenza. I have read many books that point to the evidence of life after death through the current research in quantum mechanics, particle physics, epigenetics, and the neurosciences. I have also brought these teaching to my students in my spiritual teachings classes. In this book I have not included all the new science on consciousness and brain science, but I have mentioned some studies and have included quotes from scientist, researchers, and medical doctors, wherever appropriate, to promote a clear understanding of the idea I am presenting. The topic of the union of science and spirituality is a big one and would need to be another book on its own. I have chosen to keep this book simple, yet impactful and uplifting.

I will be using the term vibrational relationship to describe the current relationship I have with Sal. The vibrational relationship is a relationship with someone who is now formless. This ability to feel and connect will be explained in Part II of this book and is interwoven throughout the book.

Throughout this book I will use the words source, infinite intelligence, presence, being, divine, self, consciousness, and unmanifested, to mean what many call God. God can be a loaded word for some and can carry lots of baggage with it. However, I will still use the word God in this book from time to time. In this book, God will never mean a white-haired man who is hanging out on a cloud, looking down on humanity to judge and punish us. When I use the word God, or any of the words I mentioned above, I will be referring to the eternal one consciousness underlying all forms of life. That which is the infinite field of all possibilities. It is all around us as well as within us. This essence cannot be described in words; it is more likely *felt in* meditation, prayer, and contemplation or in intense presence.

When I use the word ego or egoic mind, I am describing the condition of humans who are identified with *only* the body and thought forms, as who they are. The ego is never in the present moment; it only lives in thoughts of the past or future. The ego gives us a sense of separation and duality. The small self, inner critic, storyteller, and false self can all be used to describe the ego. However, we all have egos and we need our egos to maneuver in this physical reality. We just need to be careful not to place our identity in the ego, rather we need to manage our ego.

I will also use the words, true essence, soul, and spirit to describe the part of us that is a droplet of God. The formless part of us that is made in the image and likeness of God.

My wish for all who read this book is that by telling my story, it will awaken in you what you already intuitively know. The body dies, but *you* do not. You feel separated from a loved one when they pass, but you are not separate from them or anyone else. We are all connected by love. There truly is one mind, one consciousness that we are all a part of. I encourage you to be open to the possibility that grief doesn't have to overpower you. Could it be that your soul chooses everything that happens in your life, to awaken you to the ever-new consciousness that you are? Honor life as your pathway to lead you to growth and expansion, to awaken you to realize your eternal, connected, timeless Self.

Note: On the website **choosetotalwellness.org** under Book *Together Forever* you will see photos from stories in the book.

PART I:

LOST AND FOUND

CHAPTER ONE:

The Backstory

Michael

Hope is not dead, it is just larger than our imaginations: its purpose extending beyond our comprehension.

–KATHY HOBAUGH, AUTHOR

Choosing Hope, by Anna Marie Enea
~ 1993 Spring Edition of *Infinity Limited*.

My prayers had been answered. It was Halloween, 1967; my mother had given birth to a beautiful baby boy. We called him Michael. Nothing in my world could have made me happier than to have my very own baby brother. His birth affirmed my belief that children's prayers truly are answered (Part III, Chapter Nine: Prayer). I had been praying every night since I was in third grade for a baby brother or sister, and now I was in fifth grade and Michael arrived on Halloween.

Michael brought much joy to my family. Everyone loved Michael; he was an adorable little boy with an even temperament and a carefree nature. He loved to be cuddled. He was the type of child you just want to hug and hold in your arms. He had soft golden-brown curls that framed his petite face. His large hazel eyes seem to see into the depth of your soul.

Michael's presence in my life surpassed all my expectations. I had so much fun dressing him up in cute baby outfits, taking him for walks in the stroller, baby-sitting him with my best friend, taking pictures of him, and rocking him to sleep. I didn't even mind changing his diapers. Through my adolescence and teenage years, I continued to enjoy Michael's company. He was always a ray of sunshine in my life. I looked forward to coming home from school so I could play with him. He was always happy to see me. Later, when I would come home from college on the weekends, he would be outside riding his bike, popping wheelies on the vacant dirt lot adjacent to our house. He would see me drive up and jump off his bike and fly into my arms. He was always the first to greet me. As he grew older I would find him in the garage working on his dirt bikes. I would always stop and visit with him before going into the house to visit with my parents. When I was in high school and college, I enjoying taking Michael places with me. All my friends enjoy having Michael hang out with us.

Michael grew into a very independent young man. He was very athletic and became adept at many independent sports including surfing, skiing, wind surfing, scuba diving, skateboarding, and motocrossing. He was six feet two inches tall and slender but muscular. As he entered his early twenties, he grew more self-assured.

As time went by, our age difference seemed to mesh as so often happens. We shared many of the same interests. At different times in our lives we traveled throughout Europe and Southeast Asia, lived and worked in Hawaii and Pacific Grove, California and enjoyed many independent sports.

I felt so lucky to have a brother who expressed so much concern for his sister. During my pregnancies, whenever I would speak with Michael, he would always start off by asking how I was feeling. I knew he was genuinely concerned. He would inform me if he had heard some new findings concerning the health of pregnant women and their unborn babies. When my children were born, Michael was the first to arrive in the delivery room to meet the new family member. I loved the smile on his face when I asked him to be godfather for my first born, Sal.

One Saturday morning in June of 1992, at 6:00 a.m., the phone rang. I was sleeping next to my two sons. Sal was three years old, and Arthur, was only eight months old. My husband (at the time) had already left to play golf. The caller was my sister Sylvia, who told me Michael had been hurt. He was in Highland Hospital; he had been beaten up, but she knew no further details. The hospital was in a rough area, and she told me I should wait until my husband came home. I hung up. I did not think twice about waiting for him to come home. I threw some clothes on. I quickly buckled the still soundly sleeping children into their car seats and left them with my sister-in-law who lives nearby.

As I drove on I-80 toward the hospital, I was trembling; thoughts were swirling in my mind. I could not stand the thought of someone hurting my little brother. What if they had broken his nose? I'd kill them myself (Just an expression!) Michael didn't cause trouble. He was soft-spoken, kind, and gentle. But he didn't scare easily; he was not one to run or accept threats. I thought of how I had been wanting to call him so we could take our dogs walking together. He had been on my mind lately. I had a soft voice urging me to spend some quality time with him. Michael was very quiet around the family, but when it was just the two of us, he really opened up. I looked forward to our talks and really valued our closeness. I thought of how I could help him if he had to spend some time laid up and how hard that would be for him.

I thought of how handsome he looked yesterday when our family had lunch together to celebrate Sylvia's birthday. Michael had just started working full time in a new job and was able to buy some beautiful clothing. He wore an earthly blue rayon shirt, a perfect color for him. I sat next to him at lunch, and as usual, we joked around. I laughed as he teased all the nephews and nieces who loved it. I wondered if he was still wearing that blue shirt last night and if the paramedics had cut it off.

Not in my worst nightmares, did I imagine that Michael would be brain dead, and on a ventilator. But that was the harsh reality I was about to face.

The nurse led me to see Michael. He was lying on a bed. His eyes were swollen shut, his forehead was flattened and raw on one side. One of his hands were swollen; the nurse said it was used to block his face from attack. The rest of his body looked fine. He was warm and breathing. I called his name but he did not respond; at times he seemed to, but it was just a twitch. I held Michael's hand in mine; it felt warm and alive. I wanted so badly for him to wake up. But Michael was not there in that familiar body. He was gone.

My sweet baby brother had been murdered. I couldn't believe it; I didn't want to believe it. It was, sadly the truth.

My father had passed away three and a half years ago. Michael's death occurred a day after my father's birthday and a day before Father's Day. My mother had never adjusted to my father's death, I wasn't sure she could survive this blow. Michael had lived with Mom. He was her closest companion. I wondered if these killers were also inadvertently going to claim my mother's life as well. I was filled with rage, sadness, disbelief, disgust, and confusion all at the same time.

On June 19, 1992, Michael, who was then twenty-four, had gone to a benefit concert at the Scottish Rite Temple in Oakland with some friends. The couple who had driven Michael and two friends, Greg and JD, decided to leave before the end of the concert. Michael and his friends planned to call a cab. As they ventured outside the temple, they observed a group of rowdies hanging around the building, where the phone booth was. (Remember no cell phones in 1992). They decided to walk to Greg's house about a mile away, rather than standing outside waiting for a cab. Greg lived off of Grand Avenue, a yuppie area of Oakland.

They were almost at Greg's house when six men ran across the street and came up from behind Michael and his two friends. They swung at all three, but Greg and JD managed to escape. A two hundred and seventy pound, twenty-nine-year-old man hit Michael. The blow was to the back of the head. Michael fell to the ground. Once he was on the ground, the attackers began to kick him in the head repeatedly. These six men were reported to be laughing throughout the entire attack. When questioned by the homicide officers, they told them they just wanted to have some fun. Michael was killed just a week after the Rodney King riots. There was anger in the air in Oakland over these riots.

Michael's death was a senseless hate crime, which made the loss even more agonizing. His death made me despise prejudice of any kind and to have more compassion for all people who were hated on and who hated because of prejudice.

The week following Michael's death is hard to remember now. I slept maybe two or three hours a night. I was incredibly busy making arrangements for the ceremonies, working with the media, and trying my best to be supportive for my mother. The loss of Michael was unbearable, but the tragedy of his brutal death added to the already insufferable heartbreak.

I found it very ironic that the most innocent, loving, gentle person I knew would be taken in such a senseless and violent manner. Michael represented peace. He was one of the few people I know who would rarely speak badly of others. He only would state the facts and let you make your own judgment. He was an excellent listener and was always the first to help anyone in need, never worrying whether the favor would be returned. So why him?

I thought of other peaceful people who had their lives taken in violent and senseless crimes. John Lennon, Martin Luther King, Jesus Christ, Gandhi, the list goes on. I thought about how these people were teachers for us all. And I thought of how lucky I was to have Michael in my life and of how he was also a teacher for me and all those whose lives he touched.

I do not claim to understand these bizarre happenings, and I know I can't change what happened. But I do know that I have control over my own reaction to what happened. I had a choice. I could hold on to my pain and anger and direct my energy toward hating these six men and others like them or I could somehow try to turn a very negative occurrence into something positive.

To have hope for any positive change, I knew I had to react differently. I had a lot of pent-up energy, and so did many of Michael's friends. I decided to channel that energy into a positive direction. Most of his friends joined me in that endeavor. We organized some candlelight vigils and peace rallies on the corner where the homicide occurred. The media covered all of our events. We wanted to make people aware and hoped to raise some consciousness toward peace. Michael's murder was Oakland's hundred and fifth homicide of the year and it was only June. Michael was a peaceful person; I wanted his name to be remembered as something positive, not murder victim 105. I decided to create a foundation for nonviolence in his name.

I wasn't sure how I was going to accomplish this task, which seemed overwhelming at that time. Then a strange thing happened—it was as though Michael or a strong intuitive force were guiding me—everything just started falling into place. A friend of a friend told me about a community foundation that might be able to help me. Sure enough, they helped me set up the Michael Enea Memorial Fund For Non-Violence. I knew the next step was to organize a fundraiser, but where was I to start? A few days after I set up the fund, Michael's girlfriend, Claudia, called to tell me a friend's mother had called her. She had seen Claudia's name in the paper from one of our peace rallies. She owned a large private park and offered it to us for a picnic. We had just done a picnic for family and friends. The first word out of my mouth when Claudia told me this was "fundraiser." This well-known park was the perfect setting for a picnic fundraiser.

A small group of us formed a committee and created an upbeat event called "Sunday In The Park," which turned out to be a very successful fundraiser. Almost five hundred people showed up for a barbecue and old-fashioned fun in a beautiful park. Most were extended family and friends. Several concerned citizens attended, including the mayors of Oakland and San Leandro. We raised over $8,000 to start the fund. The money would go toward youth programs in the Bay Area that deal with social responsibility, conflict resolution, and interracial harmony.

(I used this seed money to create, The Michael Enea Fund for Non-Violence. It was created twenty-two years ago and is still providing donations for prevention of violence through the East Bay Community Foundation.)

Just about everything needed for the event was donated. Nobody was paid a salary, and the leftover food went straight to a nearby homeless shelter. I knew Michael was smiling that day!

It really lifted my spirits to have Michael's friends be so supportive and enthusiastic about the event. But what I found most consoling was that they really have hope for peace and harmony in the world. They are in their twenties, they are the future.

I realize everyone reacts to grief and loss differently, but if more of us could band together and try to do something positive in this crazy world, maybe we would start to see some positive change around us. Helping others is excellent therapy for all of us. And to think that what I am doing might help save someone else's loved one, makes it well worth the effort.

The ultimate motivator for me was the presence of my two young boys, only eight months and three years old. I brought them into this world and I was going to do my part to not only raise them as responsible, conscious men, but also leave this world better than I found it. I know that even the smallest acts of kindness raise the consciousness of humanity. If everyone did their part to improve our world, with time, the accumulative actions would manifest a world of peace. Peace always begins with ourselves, and like a pebble thrown in a lake, it ripples throughout the entire lake to the very edge of the shore.

What it really comes down to is choice—a choice to live with hope or with despair.

Choosing Hope

Hope is being able to see that there is light, despite all of the darkness.

–DESMOND TUTU, THEOLOGIAN

After Michael's death, I saw my mother fall into a deep sadness. The grief and depression seemed to worsen with time. She lost the sparkle in her eyes and had little enthusiasm for life. At times she seemed a little better, but the grip of depression and the loss of joy in her life always returned. She began to develop some serious health problems that worsened with time until it got to the point where she was yearning to make her own transition. Death seemed to be the only way she saw where she could be with Michael again. She had five children left on earth and twelve grandchildren, but still her will to live was slowly diminishing with each passing year, especially as her body started to fail.

After losing a child myself, I understand how this darkness can overcome you if you don't know how to break free of it. And the longer the grip of darkness holds you, the harder it is to move toward light. I lost not only my brother but also, through his death, my mother. She could not get over the pain and could not move out of the past. She would watch home movies of happier times over and over again. She never really accepted what had happened. Who could blame her for wanting to hold on to happier times and live as much as possible in the past?

I learned that the longer my mother dwelled in despair and depression, the harder it was to pull her out. At first she was more receptive and would seem a bit better, but soon she would drop into depression. I tried hard to keep her at peace but I could not get her to stay there. I learned that not only was it impossible to change some else's state of mind, but also that in attempting to raise her up, I would sometimes be brought down into low energy and sadness.

I had a family at home, which included a baby, a toddler, and a husband. I also was working and lived over an hour away from my mother. Falling into sadness would not help my mother or anyone else. It was a difficult lesson to accept and learn. I decided to consciously choose hope instead of despair. I had to provide a well-balanced, positive home for my children to thrive.

I too was dealing with the grief and loss of my brother, Michael. I learned that *only we* can bring ourselves up. Another person cannot do this for us. However, if one is open and asking for help it is possible to assist, but that person has to ultimately do the work of lifting themselves, for any real change to occur and last. I found it takes an incredibly strong, focused mind and steady healthy habits, to stay on the track of healing and growth and to guard oneself from falling into despair.

I found it helped to see my mother to her soul; she was still a very powerful, vibrant being, underneath the depressed personality. I knew that personality was not really her; I continued to see her inner light, which did have a positive affect as she seemed more at peace. It was a beautiful way to reach her.

After Michael

Grief can be the garden of compassion. If you keep your heart open through everything, your pain can become your greatest ally in your life's search for love and wisdom.

–RUMI, THIRTEENTH-CENTURY SCHOLAR AND POET

Michael's death was one of the first and strongest motivators that set me on the spiritual path. I was reading lots of spiritual books before that and dabbling in meditation, but I had no real direct experience of what I was reading about. I had a tremendous amount of spiritual growth through Michael's transition. These leaps of spiritual growth continued throughout the years and many times I saw them originating from the loss of Michael.

My mother was very religious and intuitive. Even though my mother also had so many amazing signs from Michael, she never realized that she could continue a vibrational relationship with him. At the time of Michael's transition, I also never knew this could be a reality for me. Also, when one is in fear and depression, we quickly forget the incredible signs and the feeling of awe that accompanies the signs. We may even brush them off as some odd coincidence or a trick of the imagination. As one becomes more depressed, it becomes more difficult to be open to the signs or even notice them.

What I *observed* through my mother's experience is that if you lose a child, you suffer for the rest of your life—you get sick and you finally leave the planet. You miss the person, and the only way you see to be reunited with them is through death. Or you don't know what to believe, so accepting one's death is nearly impossible.

However, what I *learned* from my mother is different from what I *observed*. I learned that I never would want to fall into a deep depression, leading to illness and possibly death. No matter what happened in my life, I was going to accept it and learn from it and use it for growth, for awakening. I had already read many spiritual books that taught me there was a different way to deal with what the personality calls tragedy and the soul calls life lessons for growth. When we learn that there is another way, we are empowered. We learn that we can choose love over fear.

I observed how I felt when my mother forgot my birthday, but mourned for the entire month of Michael's birthday. I learned from that experience that I could never do that to a child of mine. I did not feel sad because she forgot my birthday; I understood that she was in severe pain. I felt sad because I felt helpless to assist her to find a way out of her intense pain. I felt sad that celebrating my birthday or another family member's birthday could no longer give her the joy it once did. It was completely heartbreaking to witness this, but even worse, it was awful to feel helpless to relieve her from this horrible pain she chronically endured.

I have always known that for me the worst thing that could happen would be to lose a child. I felt that might just be an unbearable challenge for me. I was not sure I would have the will to live after something so tragic, especially after witnessing my mother's life. Losing a child was the one thing, as a spiritual teacher, in which I was not sure I could walk my talk. Being a mother came natural to me. I loved becoming a mother and saw it as the most important responsibility I would ever take on. I view motherhood as a sacred honor.

I have to say that even though I lost my brother, Michael, and saw how horrible it was for my mother, I never carried any conscious fear of it actually happening to me, and yet it did. Michael and my son, Sal, both left this earth, unexpectedly, at the young age of just twenty-four years old.

The Tragic Night

Truly, it is in the darkness that one finds the light, so when we are in the sorrow, then this light is nearest of all to us.

–MEISTER ECKHART, THIRTEENTH-CENTURY GERMAN PHILOSOPHER

It is hard to write about the most heartbreaking moment of your life. But, for the purpose of helping others through the loss of a loved one, I will attempt here to describe the night I lost my incredibly beloved son, Sal.

It was an unusually warm, balmy Monday afternoon on November 25, 2013, when I got a call from Sal. I had just walked Rosie, the family dog, on the beach in northern California where I live. I was getting ready to cook dinner before teaching yoga that evening. He wanted to get together, but I told him I had to teach and invited him to come for dinner later. He agreed and I was excited that he was coming over. I immediately ran to the grocery store to get all the ingredients to make one of his favorite dinners. When Sal came over for dinner, it meant an evening of laughter, interesting conversations, and hearing about some new adventure he had done or was planning on doing. Sal had a special way of lifting my spirits and making me feel enthusiastic to be alive. I was grateful that Sal always lived close by. San Francisco was only about forty minutes from our home. He went to college there and continued to live there after college.

After getting home from teaching my usual Monday night yoga class that evening and getting ready for Sal to come, I sat down and joined my husband, who was watching *Downtown Abbey* on TV. Rosie immediately jumped on my lap and curled up. A feeling of warmth and contentment stirred in me, as I sat with the family, enjoying the aroma from the kitchen of a home-cooked meal. It was one of those days where everything went well and life felt really good. Knowing that Sal would be over any minute now, was the highlight for me. I had no idea that what was to happen next would change our lives forever.

I got a call from Lauren, Sal's girlfriend of many years. She was gasping for air, sobbing, and telling me that Sal was in a motorcycle accident near Devil's Slide on Highway 1. I was trying to understand what she was saying. My heart dropped, my throat closed up, and I felt frozen—frozen in time and frozen in my body. I only heard words like motorcycle, fire, ambulance, and San Francisco General Hospital. Lauren was following Sal in her car as he rode his motorcycle. To this day I am so thankful that Lauren was not on the motorcycle with him, but she was there, to pull him out of the fire and hold him in her arms and comfort him as the ambulance was coming.

My husband and I, immediately got in the car and headed to the hospital. As we were driving there, I was breathing deep and doing my best to stay calm and present. I knew I needed to do this not only for me but also for my husband. For a spilt second, the thought of Michael passing at twenty-four and Sal being twenty-four popped into my head. But I immediately dismissed it. We arrived at San Francisco General Hospital, as we drove up and parked, the ambulance crew awkwardly glanced at us. I suspected Sal might have already been gone. Once in the reception area of the emergency room, they gave us the run-around, again with the look on their faces, I feared he was either gone or almost gone. I did my best to push the thought of Sal dying out of my mind, but sometimes our intuition is so strong and especially between a mother and child, that the feeling cannot be denied, yet hope reigned as my predominant emotion for now.

I felt sick to my stomach, my head began to spin and my whole body felt so weak. I felt I might collapse, but I needed to be strong, to find my son in this hospital. Where was he and why were they not taking us to him? They eventually put us in a small room with a social worker, again a bad sign. But still, I had hope. Maybe, I was just being paranoid. But my body was having such a strong, almost violent, reaction, it knew the truth.

I left and went to the bathroom, and when I came out I was disoriented and didn't know where I was. I knew my entire being was going into shock. I knew I wasn't fully in my body, I felt as though I wasn't grounded, but was fluttering somewhere between my body and the space above my head. I finally demanded that if my son was in the hospital taking his last breath I wanted to be there NOW.

Shortly after that a young male doctor came in and blurted out the awful news, I knew was coming. He said there was nothing they could do to save him. Sal had died, he was GONE. I now felt myself lift completely out of my body and watched the scene from above—it felt surreal. It was abrupt and as sudden as could be, with no chance for a goodbye or a last hug or kiss. I did not want to come back into my body; I simply could not handle this news. But I knew I had to, I had to be strong for my husband and for the people who loved Sal and mostly for my younger son, Arthur, who had no life experiences or tools to handle such a devastating blow. Sal and Arthur had been inseparable throughout their entire lives. They were closer than most brothers; they were best friends. Arthur had never conceived of a life without Sal. I had to be strong for Arthur. But I did not want to be strong. I did not want to accept this devastating news. I wanted to be the one who died. I did not want to live a life without Sal in it.

The social worker led us down a cold and dingy hospital hallway to an empty, dark room where Sal laid on a gurney that was against the far wall. The social worker barely let us see him; it was just for a few moments and they would not let us touch him. They had him covered with a white sheet up to his neck. He had been wearing his huge helmet that I bought him the day he got his bike. So his face looked perfect, apart from a slight bruise on his right cheekbone. His long, wavy hair was flowing over the edge of the table, where he laid. He looked beautiful and peaceful. He looked like Saint Michael the Archangel. Because his skin was smooth and his profile was well-defined and strong like Saint Michael. The white sheet looked like a white gown that an angel would wear. I wanted to hug his body and hold him close to me. But the social worker told us again we were not allowed to touch him; she stayed with us, hovering from behind. I stood as close as I could to him and could feel his body was still warm as I brushed against his side. But I did as I was instructed. I was in deep shock and disbelief at that point. It felt hard to move my body or even think. What difference would it have made to them if I held Sal in my arms? And it would have given me something that I needed at that moment, a last hug from Sal.

But as you continue to read, you will see that I get my hugs from Sal in a much more alive, real, and vivid way.

I knew I had to be focused to support my husband, who was filled with rage and shock. We had to go to Sal and Arthur's house, to let Arthur know firsthand, the devastating news and to take him home with us. Sal and Arthur lived together and worked together in San Francisco. I had to tell Arthur that his one and only sibling, his big brother, Sal was gone. Arthur only knew life with Sal, there was never a moment of his entire life that Sal was not part of.

When Arthur opened the door and saw our faces, he knew something terrible had happened. He immediately thought our dog, Rosie, had died. As sad as that would have been, I wished it were the bad news we had to deliver. Arthur is the sweetest soul I have ever known, much like my brother Michael. He is the kind of child you just want to protect from pain. And now I had to give him news that I feared would be an unbearable pain for him to endure. Losing Sal was beyond comprehension, and in the same night, we had to give our only child left, news that could possibly affect him for the rest of his life. Life was feeling like too much burden to bear. I truly wished it was me who had gone, not Sal. I had lived enough life, Sal had not, but the divine order of the universe had Sal making his transition at this time, not me. There was nothing I could do about it.

Arthur had a hard time believing the heart-wrenching news, to be true. For Sal had seemed invincible to all of us, but especially to Arthur. Arthur kept saying, "Are you sure?" Not in our wildest dreams did any of us think something could take the invincible, larger-than-life, street-smart, Sal from us. He was strong, athletic, extremely smart, and emotionally well-balanced. Sal was tender and loving and so authentic. He was someone you could trust with your deepest secret or your greatest possession. Arthur immediately became physically ill, vomiting and becoming physically weak.

Sal had always taken Arthur under his wing, and since the day Arthur was born, Sal had adored him and wanted to be with him. When I was pregnant with Arthur, I would let Sal put his hand on my belly and he could feel his future baby brother moving. Sal and I would sing sweet lullabies to Arthur while he was still in my womb. Sal had an immediate love for Arthur and loved taking care of him and teaching him new things. And Arthur looked up to Sal and loved him with all his heart. Sal was only two years and nine months older than Arthur, but Sal was always light years ahead of his age so it was natural for him to look out for his little brother. Sal and Arthur never argued either; I was truly blessed as a mother of two boys who just simply got along. This may sound like an exaggeration, but it is the truth.

We took Arthur home with us. I wanted to sit in the backseat with Arthur and soothe him and wrap my arms around him. But Chuck was so distraught, everyone deals with tragedy in his or her own way. As the matriarch of the family I felt torn between soothing my son and calming my husband. What I realize now, is that I should have been taking care of myself. If I did I would have followed my heart and went in the backseat with Arthur. I needed to be hugged and held as well. And my maternal instinct to help my only physical child was almost overpowering.

I needed to call Lauren, Sal's girlfriend, who was on her way to the hospital; she had to stay behind at the accident scene to answer questions for the police. It broke my heart that she was not allowed to go in the ambulance with Sal, she could have been with him to hold his hand as he made his transition. Lauren is like the daughter I never had, we are very close. Lauren was only twenty-one and I knew this news would be devastating for her. My husband did not want me to call anyone; this was understandable because speaking the words made it more real and he was not ready to accept this awful truth yet. But I knew Lauren was driving to the hospital and I absolutely had to call her. I told her that no visitors were allowed and she needed to go home immediately. But she would not listen and said she was going there anyway. I told her to pull over and was forced to tell her the awful news that I think she intuitively already knew in her heart. Sal was gone, Sal had died in the motorcycle accident. Again my heart broke into pieces with the responsibility to be the messenger of this crushing news. I am an empath, meaning I easily feel other people's pain; this night was killing me over and over again. Lauren stayed put on the side of the road until her girlfriend picked her up and took her home.

Moving Into Acceptance

If you find your life situation unsatisfactory or even intolerable, it is only by surrendering (acceptance) first that you can break the unconscious resistance pattern that perpetuates that situation. It is precisely at these times that surrender needs to be practiced to eliminate pain and sorrow from your life.

–ECKHART TOLLE, AUTHOR—POWER OF NOW

When we got home, we picked up Rosie and we all got into our king-size bed. My heart was aching not only for myself, but also for my family, Lauren, and all of Sal's friends who loved him dearly. I was filled with compassion for everyone who was going to be affected by the loss of Sal. How were any of us going to be able to go on without Sal? Sal was in many ways becoming the leader of our family, he was at the point where he was organizing some of our vacations and holidays. He brought so much fun into our family. How would this affect Arthur's young life? Going from an incredible brotherhood, where the two lived, worked, and played together, to being an only child. And then there was my husband, who was also devastated. Was he going to be able to cope with life again? I really thought I might not make it through the night; this was just all too much to bear.

As Chuck, Arthur, and Rosie lay in bed, I knew I could not sleep. A strong inner pull guided me to light a candle; the only one I could see in our bedroom was a beautiful golden candle of the Buddha's head. It was the kind of candle you do not light because the candle itself is a piece of artwork. But I knew that was the one to light. Sal was not religious but he was spiritual in his own way, the Buddha inspired him, so it seemed quite perfect.

I lit the candle and I sat up in bed all night and into the daylight of morning. I knew I needed to sit in meditation; be still and tune in to the wisdom of my soul. My soul was already guiding me to meditate. It was crystal clear that I needed to accept what happened. I knew for sure that I had to feel the pain fully; I had to allow the pain to penetrate to the bottom of my heart, into my entire being. I had to feel it and then let it pass through me. It was important to fully embrace the pain, to fully accept and surrender unto the most unbearable pain I could ever imagine. But I also knew once I accepted and fully felt it, I did not need to hold on to the pain. But with a loss like this, would the pain ever subside? Would I be living in constant pain? I didn't even know at this time if acceptance would do anything, I just knew I had to accept. Every fiber of my being was pulling me to sit in stillness and allow the Higher Intelligence to take over, my ego needed to let go and go away for now.

I had to accept what had happened. I knew that if I did not accept, I would block the pain and go into denial and I would suffer for a long time. If I denied what happened on any level, it would never go away. If I did fully accept now, maybe in the long run, I would not suffer and there would be hope for healing. I thought that if I sat and meditated on acceptance of the situation, it might actually kill me. I knew I could possibly suffer a heart attack, but quite frankly, that was a risk I knew I had to take. I could not change what had happened, and it was not going to get better. I had to accept what was. As I went into this meditation on acceptance, it felt as though I was literally jumping off a cliff, and as far as I was concerned, I had no choice in the matter. So I ran with all my might with determination to stay present in meditation and I jumped off the cliff into acceptance.

I knew I had to accept only this one thing: the physical Sal was gone. I did *not* think of him as a seed I grew in my womb and whom I witnessed every moment of his life as he grew into the most adorable baby, to a cuddly toddler, a bright-eyed child, an adventurous adolescent, an athletic teen, and a handsome, optimistic, talented, kind young man. That would have been too hard and too much past. In this meditation, I knew I just had to accept this moment, no moments behind me or in front of me, just the moment I'm in *now*. I did have to accept that his physicality as I knew him was forever vanished from the earth.

I knew that if I did *not* accept this fact, I would suffer indefinitely. I knew accepting this fact I would also suffer, but maybe not indefinitely. I was careful to focus on only the one fact—Sal was physically gone. I did not project stories in my head of how anyone else would be affected or how my life would be horrible from now on. No, I did not let one thought in, other than the fact that Sal in his physicality was gone. At this time, I did not even try to connect with his being. I knew that could not be possible anyway until I came into acceptance. I did not clutter my mind with any other thoughts; I got those out of the way. It was easier to quiet my mind, to sit in complete stillness, and just focus on my breath without the storyteller making its commentary. By the very nature of the incident, I was forced into the most alert stillness I have ever known. I knew exactly what I needed to do from the guidance of my soul, from all my spiritual studies, my daily practice of meditation/mindfulness and yoga. And that was to sit in stillness until I fully accepted what had happened.

As I sat in silent stillness and accepted this painful truth, I was fully aware that my brain and my body had suffered shock. I mean physically suffered from shock. I felt as though I had a skull cap on, that was squeezing my head and brain. My body felt as though I had been beaten up. I felt very weak physically and completely drained emotionally. I was aware of it, but I did not make any more of it than knowing it was there.

The golden yellow Buddha candle burned well into the daylight hours of the next day. I never moved from the glowing protection of the golden light coming from the Buddha candle. Sitting, breathing, and staying present while all the time moving deeper and deeper into acceptance. The normal thoughts of "Why me?" and "This wasn't supposed to happen!" never entered my mind that night, nor have they ever entered my mind after that meditation of complete acceptance.

In my meditation, sitting in stillness, in the silence of the night, those hours after losing Sal in the physical, I did not attempt to soothe myself in anyway. That first night, I put all my focus on one conscious breath at a time. I did not need to accept stories about anything, no, just this present moment. If I let my mind wander into fear-based thoughts about the accident, I could really snowball into darkness and despair.

All of the spiritual teachings that I had been studying, practicing, and teaching for years, were now priceless in my healing process and my reaction to Sal's transition. I had practiced for years to move into stillness and silence and to let it take me from thinking to a place of just *being* and *feeling*. There were long periods of absolutely no thought.

As I began to meditate, my body finally began to relax, as if the golden light of the burning candle was also within me, warming my tense muscles and illuminating my essence. The personality, the thinker was gone. I was not aware of time, I was not aware of "me." I felt as though the light of Consciousness had transported me to a different dimension of timeless Being. After hours of this deep meditation, I forgot where I was and who I was. Being forced into this intense state of presence, a deep inner peace finally came over me. This inner peace was not of this material world, but from the formless realm. It was a peace that was different, it was a peace that was new to me. It felt like it could be the peace that Jesus spoke of, the peace of God that surpasses all understanding. Because it was hard to understand how I could feel peaceful with my heart broken into a million pieces, and yet there was this intense underlying peace that held me like a loving mother's embrace.

Sometimes when something so hugely tragic happens to us, something much larger and much more powerful than us, takes us over. With my eyes closed in meditation and focused upward at the brow center, I saw a bright indigo light, with a white light in the shape of a five-pointed star at the center. This light was emanating from the brow center and engulfing me; the light came with a loving presence that is hard to describe in words other than to say, it felt like unconditional love. I sometimes see this indigo light in meditation, but is not as bright and engulfing. Only once before had I *felt it* as such a strong, protective, loving presence—the night I lost my brother, Michael. Could this light, protection, and love be what is called the "Grace of God"? I believe it is. It blows in at a time when you just don't know if you can go on. I feel acceptance allows this grace to be released and infused into every cell of my being, right down to my core.

The grace of God is a wind which is always blowing.

−Sri Ramakrishna

What happened was, once I fully accepted the unbearable truth, that my son, Sal, was dead. Something deep within me opened. I would say in the heart if I had to pinpoint a physical area of the opening. The heart had cracked open, leaving a vast spaciousness for something new to enter my being. At first, I just felt a huge void in my heart, but as the days passed, I began to feel my entire being fill with compassion, love, grace, and serenity. It wasn't just a feeling of peace and love being in me, it was *who I was, who I am.* I also felt an underlying love in everyone else, even if it was a difficult person in my life. It felt like I was not alone, that I was loved beyond measure, that I was seen and understood by a loving Presence much greater than myself.

I knew deep in my being that separation and death were just conceptual ideas in our heads, that we all bought into, but that in reality there was no separation and no ending to us, no death. Yes, there was physical death, but we are not these bodies. We are timeless, eternal spiritual beings. Further, each one of us is a droplet of the underlying consciousness (God) that makes all things possible. I realized on a deep level that life just keeps on going and that actually we don't have a life, rather we are life.

I knew what was real, was my love for Sal and his love for me and that love and connection were constant and could not be threatened in any way. And not only is our love real, but are Essence is real. Neither our love for one another nor our true Essence could be drowned, stabbed, shot, or threatened in anyway. Our love and who we truly are could never be destroyed! And I knew that unconditional love was who we all are at our core. And the *one unconditional love*, which we are all part of, was what we call Source or God. Hence, it was at this moment, that I began to have the courage to live my life by what *A Course In Miracles* (a spiritual text), teaches.

Nothing real can be threatened.
Nothing unreal exists.
Herein lies the peace of God. (T-in.2) *A Course in Miracles*

I knew I had taken a risk of physically dying from the heartbreak, if I meditated on acceptance so soon. When the normal thing to do for survival was to go into denial. But it did not kill my physical body; this deep acceptance transcended the pain into deep inner peace, and with time meaning. It softened the ego and freed the spirit in me. The acceptance did not transform the situation, the fact that Sal's physicality was gone, it *transformed me* so that I was able to awaken to a deeper inner peace and an understanding that in the big picture of life and in the greater reality, *all is well and in divine order.*

I was still in pain from the loss of my son; there was a hole in my heart the size of the Grand Canyon. But healing was already occurring, and without acceptance, there would be no healing, and pain in the form of anger, denial, depression, and disease would most likely pursue.

However, it took years for me to realize what had really happened that first night—during that ten-hour intense meditation of acceptance. In the experience of writing this book I received more clarity of what happened that night and in the days that followed. I journaled daily during this time, mostly about my feelings, as I read these notes from years ago at the time of Sal's death. It became very evident that a strong transcendence had occurred, stemming from the courage to go directly into acceptance. Sometimes when we step back we can see with great clarity, then when we are in the middle of it. When we are in the middle of it, we are just taking one day at a time, and sometimes, even one breath at a time, as I did during this meditation. The clarity is easily available in reflection, years after the event. Hence, the saying "hindsight is 2020" is a well-known fact.

In the days and weeks after Sal's transition, my heart continued to swell with love, even though the sadness was also there. I could not think a negative thought about anyone. I felt this incredible connection to everyone and everything. I felt the underlying oneness of it all, pervading my life experience.

I knew most people thought I was in denial because I was in a place of deep peace and love after Sal's transition; however, I never lost that gift.

My students and a few close friends were the only ones who really knew I was not in denial. Because they knew me, what I practiced, what I taught, and they saw my teaching coming from a deeper level of awareness, after Sal's passing.

With all of this, it is extremely important to realize that acceptance does not take away the pain of loss immediately. TThe pain and shock of the tragic loss was still there, but with acceptance came peace and I knew I had a chance to heal. Without acceptance, the tragedy of this night would forever live deeply buried in my psyche and would emerge at weak moments. Without acceptance, my life would be lived in a dysfunctional manner, going into guilt, anger, depression, blame, self-pity, isolation, and so forth. With acceptance, I had a chance at becoming whole again. And I knew this was the best thing I could do for my loved ones, as well as myself.

With time, acceptance led me to see *meaning* in Sal's death, I learned some invaluable life lessons. Through the pain of loss, I learned on a very deep level that nothing could take away the deep love between Sal and I, and that life continues and we are able to maintain and even grow our relationship with one another. I understood that there was a sacred contract between us, and I lost my fear of death. The greatest lesson I learned from Sal's death is that there simply is *no death* and *no separation.* I began to realize that most of our human problems occur when we see ourselves as separate from one another and disconnected from the whole.

I discovered that acceptance brought me to a deep peace as I mentioned above, and this happened right away. This deep inner *peace* brought me to express *gratitude* for the honor of having Sal as my son and to experience a love so big and so deep, I knew this love between us was a rarity. Over time, the gratitude and peace brought me back to *joy.* So to clarify, **acceptance** led to a deep inner **peace**, which led to an expression of **gratitude**, which finally accumulated in **joy.** These all came with acceptance and are priceless gifts of acceptance. But the greatest gift of acceptance is that it cracked open the door, to realizing who I truly am. The door opened just a crack that night, enough to solidify on a deeper level that there is no death and I felt who I truly was, an infinite, invisible being and so was everyone else. But I have found that, yes the door did crack open, but I need to keep opening it by my practice of presence, which is described in Part III. I found that drama and getting too busy and preoccupied with life's difficulties shut that door and I can forget all that I realized that night and beyond, whereas if I take the time to be alone in nature, if I take the time for prayer and meditate, the time to relax, the door opens again (Part III). My practice is to keep it opening further and further; this for me is the greatest adventure of life and I feel it is why we are here. It seems that opening the door is endless, there is always more to realize and discover about consciousness. Earth life can be called a giant classroom for souls to develop.

From past encounters with deceased loved ones and from the ten-hour meditation, I realized that Sal's soul had chosen to leave earth, that his purpose for this life was complete, and that Sal was in a safe place. I knew intuitively he was in our real home, which is not earth. I knew Sal was safe and really, that is all a mother really wants for her child, to be safe, happy, and alive. I knew the burden would be on me, to learn how to live without Sal in my life. This seemed like an impossible feat to me, but knowing Sal was safe made it possible for me to accept his sudden death. Most mothers prefer to take the burden in order to protect their children from suffering. I trusted the divine order of the Infinite Intelligence. And only two days later, these intuitive knowings were validated, as you will see in Chapter Two.

Love and More Love

Love recognizes no barriers. It jumps hurdles, and leaps fences, penetrates walls to arrive at its destination full of hope.

–MAYA ANGELOU

In the days that followed, I slowly emerged into a space of peace, love, compassion, and presence. At the same time, I felt the enormous void in my heart, open, raw, and unbelievably sad. The following days and nights are still somewhat of a blur, of a dream-like state.

The house was full of family and friends for several weeks after Sal's passing.

Our small local community, was so supportive of us. I never thought of the benefits of living in a small, close-knit community before, but was so grateful that I had lived in a caring community since my children were just toddlers. Sal had so many friends they seemed to be coming from everywhere. We thought we knew most of his friends, but we met many for the first time as they came over to mourn with us. Our house was right in the heart of our small town. In years past, many of Sal's friends came to our house after school from first grade on, so they are like family to us. We have seen these young men and women grow up. Our home was filled with Sal's friends from childhood, high school, college, and beyond. It was evident his friends loved him deeply and could not bear the thought of life without him. To see these grown men sitting around my dining room table weeping was hard for me, but at the same time, there was an exquisite beauty to it. To witness their courage to weep openly and to sit together with one another. We all comforted each other by just being together and sharing our love for Sal.

When people entered our home for the first time since the accident, I would hug each one of them for a long time as we shook from head to toe, weeping and grieving the loss of a bright light from our lives. But in reality all that was gone was his body, that bright light is even brighter now as it reaches so many in a different way.

The outpouring of love from our family, friends, students, and the community at large was beautiful. I was overwhelmed with the love pouring in. I could literally feel the love flowing into our family from the many prayers and healing energy that was being showered upon us. Every time I opened our front door, there was food, flowers, or a gift from a caring student, neighbor, or friend. Our mailbox was overflowing with cards. Even strangers stepped up to console us. One woman who read about Sal's death in the newspaper was a filmmaker and volunteered to film the celebration of life and more and made a video for us. A local contractor, who was a complete stranger, took the lead to work on his free weekends for months to build the yurt we dedicated to Sal as a sanctuary of peace. Many high school students who Sal mentored in the inner city of San Francisco wrote us emails of love and support. This outpouring of love helped our family tremendously; without this love pouring in, it would have been so much harder. I believe without this love coming from the outside world into our home, healing would have been prolonged and maybe even impossible. The love took away the feeling of being alone and of being a victim and made it possible for us to heal and grow from this devastating trauma. The love made us feel safe and nurtured, which gave us strength for healing.

My sisters and girlfriends were making food for us and for everyone at the house. Sal's friends got our juicer out and were making nutritious juice for us because eating was still hard. I didn't even go into my kitchen to prepare food for at least a week. I only hung out in the kitchen to share Sal stories with all our guests. I spent all my time being loved and loving.

Sal's friends rallied around us, never leaving us alone. They brought pictures of Sal and many candles over to the house. On several of the evenings following the days after Sal's passing, we went out in the front yard and placed the pictures and candles on the front lawn. We held hands in a circle around the pictures and candles and said prayers for Sal and shared words of inspiration. It was bittersweet; there was a delicate and tender beauty to the outpouring of kindness and love. We all felt the presence of Sal so strong; it was a presence of pure, unconditional love. Even though it was a time of heartbreak, it was also a sacred time of empathy, and shared love. One thing was creating this togetherness, compassion and love for one another, that one thing was our shared love for this human being who loved you so deep and saw your goodness, even when you didn't.

CHAPTER TWO:

Sal's Download

About Sal

In Sal's short life he lived more than most people do in ninety years! And if you met Sal for only 30 seconds you would remember him.

–ARTHUR ENEA O'BRIEN, SAL'S YOUNGER BROTHER

During those days after Sal made his transition, all I wanted to do was talk about Sal and hear stories from all of the people he touched in so many inspiring ways. Sal was friends with everyone, from the college professor to the drug addict; age, race, profession, and gender was no barrier to Sal, he loved people. I was touched that so many of his friends told me Sal was their best friend.

I loved hearing so many stories about Sal that I did not know. Sal and I were close; we shared so much of our lives with one another, so hearing these new stories were fascinating to me. I received emails from high school students he had counseled in Hunters Point, while he was attending University of San Francisco (USF), thanking him for working with them on core studies and encouraging them to go to college. Hunters Point is a neighborhood in the San Francisco projects. A neighbor recently told me they saw him in a documentary at a class they took at San Francisco State

University, encouraging a college education. I have to add in here that Sal did not think college was good for everyone. In fact, I had to encourage him to go college, after taking some time off after high school he did go to college.

I realized he was quiet about all the ways he touched and helped so many people. I heard so many stories of how he helped his friends in so many different ways. He helped one friend financially get through college. He helped several others realize what their passion was and inspired them to start their own unique businesses. One man he inspired was a young man who just got released from prison, another was a graduate from USF, and many others from all walks of life.

He uplifted everyone's life he came in contact with. I learned Sal was quick to forgive others, when he was wronged. Sal was one of the few people I knew who could actually see beyond your ego to your true essence. He saw the good in people and related to them from that place. Even if a person hurt or betrayed Sal, he still focused on the good in that person, which inspired that person to be better.

Sal loved to be generous with the people he cherished. When it came time to give gifts for birthdays, Christmas, Mother's Days, and other holidays he really put thought into what gift would delight you the most and gave you something that was just perfect for you. He had this trait as a small child. We live one block from Main Street, which is filled with unique little boutiques. When he was only around eight years old, he took the $20 he had gotten from his Nana on his birthday and bought me a beautiful candle for my birthday that cost $20. The storekeeper knew me and did not charge him tax. He did this on his own. The store was only half a block from our house. He dragged Arthur with him and told me it was from both of them. They were both so excited to give me this precious gift.

Sal played football at two Catholic schools in the San Francisco Bay Area. He was a gifted quarterback. I loved watching him play; he would often throw a pass or ran in the ball to bring the team to victory in the last seconds of the game. Whatever sport Sal was playing he saw his teammates as his brothers. This was especially true of football, since that was the sport he got locked into as a freshman in high school. At both schools, Sal was awarded with the honors of VIP and highest academic player for football.

Sal received many awards in his short life. Yes, he was an A student and a star athlete, but he worked hard and for long hours to be the best at whatever his endeavor was at the time. Sal was a highly motivated individual and had a strong inner drive to do and be his best. He was not competitive in the sense that he wanted to be the best and beat everyone else. He just wanted to be his personal best and he wanted to make us proud too.

One of the first awards Sal received was for running the most laps in a Jog-A-Thon to raise money for his elementary school. At only nine years old, he outran all the ten-, eleven-, and twelve-year-olds. He did this out of sheer determination. I kept telling him to slow down every time he passed me on his laps around the track. I was afraid he was going to have a heart attack!

He was awarded a special guarantee admission to one of the University of California schools. Only one student per school in the eleventh grade receives this honor. Sal also received awards for being the top student in mathematics. He would forget to tell me about these awards; the school would have to call me to make sure we showed up for awards night. These awards did not faze Sal. And in reality, they were nice, but the true blessing of Sal was simply his ability to love you so BIG and to see you right to your soul. His enthusiasm for life is what I loved best about Sal. His high vibe was contagious; he had the element of fun in him, like no one I have ever known.

When challenges came up in his life, rather than letting them take him down, he used them for growth. When he was just a junior in high school, he got recruited for quarterback at Harvard and most of the Ivy League schools. We visited many of them before he was even a senior. He got injured early in his senior year from football and was not able to play in college. I thought he would be devastated. I was very concerned how this would affect him. One day, shortly after it was evident that he would not be able to play the game he loved so much, I went into his bedroom to talk to him. He was writing the lyrics for a song. He simply said, "Mom don't worry, this is an opportunity for me to explore my love of music." Which he did. He ended up having fun in college and beyond by making some CDs and collaborating with other artists and performing at small clubs in San Francisco. He never ceased to amaze me with his positive attitude and fun-loving spirit.

Sal was truthful, authentic, sincere, and extremely adventurous. He would stress me out with his double backward flips while wakeboarding or snowboarding. I was glad his coaches weren't around to see him!

In his twenty-four years, he learned and evolved so quickly. It was like he came to earth and was on an accelerated program. If I did not see him for a week, when I did he looked different, he looked older. At two years old, we had intelligent conversations. I remember random people who could hear our conversations, ask in disbelief how old is that kid?

When he was younger he was more serious and very conscientious, and as he grew older he started really enjoying life, he became more relaxed. The last year of his life he had a premonition that he was going to die young. He realized the importance of relationships and valued family and friends more than anything. He went through phases quickly in life, always learning from his mistakes.

This short segment on Sal, barely touches on his twenty-four years, but it is enough to get an idea of who he was. But in a nutshell, Sal was all heart.

Maybe the greatest testimonial to demonstrate this statement that Sal was all heart and touched so many was the sheer numbers of attendees at his celebration of life service. I rented one of the largest spaces on the coast. It was a large hotel with several spacious ballrooms. I rented two of these large adjoining ballrooms and still the hallway was filled with friends who could not fit into the ballrooms. I would like to add that our community really stepped up and made this celebration possible for us, especially the owners of this beautiful hotel. We estimate that there were approximately five hundred people at Sal's Celebration of Life. The service went on for hours, the longest part being friends and family who stood in line at the podium to speak of their love and admiration for Sal. They spoke beautiful words of how he touched their lives and told humorous stories about Sal. The actual celebration went on all night as many rented rooms at the hotel.

To this day we still gather on Sal's birthday and celebrate him as he continues to be part of our lives. Sal still brings us all together every year on December 12. And he still brings in the element of fun in our lives by his funny and timely signs.

Sal was not the biggest guy on the field, but he had the biggest heart!

−Teammate from Riordan High School football team

The Message in the Sand

A broken heart is not the same as sadness. Sadness occurs when the heart is stone cold and lifeless. On the contrary, there is an unbelievable amount of vitality in a broken heart.

−Elizabeth Lesser, Founder of Omega Institute

Sal made his exit from earth on a Monday evening. It was a beautiful warm, balmy day on the California coast, especially for late November. That day I was enjoying walking our dog, Rosie, on the beach. I was walking on the packed wet sand, close to where the waves break. When I saw a quote in the sand. It was unusual, because it was written in perfect calligraphy. It looked fresh, as if it had just been written. Yet there was only one other person on the whole beach besides me and she was sunbathing quite far from the message. The message read:

Tears and a broken heart, make for the biggest heart

−Anonymous

I thought the quote was interesting, but it really did not apply to me, as my life was in a good flow at that time. It wasn't until a day or two after losing Sal that I remembered seeing that message in the wet sand and I knew it was meant for me. The person who wrote it, obviously did not write it for me, but the universe made sure I saw it. Whoever wrote it, did it at the perfect timing for me to witness it. It was close to the waves in the wet packed sand, but had not been washed away yet. It was probably there for a short time as it was still in perfect condition.

I found out for myself the truth of that message. As strange as it seems, after Sal passed, my heart was full of unconditional love and compassion, like never before. I have always felt I had an open heart but it was now literally cracked open and raw. It left a huge hole in my being, but that spaciousness allowed for something more sacred to fill in. For a long time after Sal passed I did not have one harmful thought. My heart had broken open and there were constant tears. The human part of me was weeping and sad, yet my wise soul was experiencing a spaciousness for something new to come in. What came in was deep inner peace and deep compassion. The bridge that connects earth to heaven, physical to nonphysical, was beginning to illuminate.

The Message in the Forest

An early morning walk is a blessing for the whole day

–Henry David Thoreau, Author, Poet, Philosopher

The most clear, vivid, and significant experience I had those days following Sal's transition was when I went for a walk in the forest. Sal passed on November 25th, the Monday evening before Thanksgiving, and one month before Christmas. Not to mention, both Sal and I have our birthdays in mid-December, only four days apart from one another.

On Wednesday, two days after Sal passed, my friend, Gail, called and told me during her morning meditation that Sal had come to her and told her to tell me to go for a walk in the forest. Gail is an extremely intuitive person and a long-time meditator, I knew she spoke the truth.

It was early in the day, but the house was already beginning to fill with friends. I told my family that I was going for a walk and would be back later. I slipped out the back door and drove to the redwood forest, which is about thirteen minutes away from our home. On most days I get up early and walk amongst the majestic redwoods. I can't think of a better way to start my day. For me a morning walk in the forest is truly a blessing for the whole day. It clears my mind and uplifts my entire being. It is a sacred space for me. It is the place that connects me with spirit more than any other place in the world. I love to walk by myself amongst the giant redwood trees.

In the forest I feel peaceful, guided, loved, and protected. I usually come out of the forest feeling energized, happy, and relaxed. On many days, it is my morning meditation. I was so grateful that Gail had called; I really needed to be alone in the forest, as I had not had much alone time outside of the ten-hour meditation, just two nights ago.

Before I entered the forest and while parked at the trailhead parking lot, I listen to a song that Sal and Arthur had written for me. I wondered, could I handle hearing his voice? Again I was taking a risk of breaking open my heart more, from hearing Sal sing to me and tell me how much I mean to him. But once again I jumped off the cliff, and listened to the song. As expected, I burst into tears as I heard him singing, "Mom, we'll be together as long as forever!" This is retold in Part II under, *The Precious and Precocious Birthday Song.*

When one enters our local forest, it feels like you are entering into a green tunnel and disappearing into a make-believe world of the utmost beauty. As you begin walking on the soft dirt path, it leads you to an entrance where the trees begin to get closer together. The branches meet overhead, providing a canopy of green redwood needles above and soft deep reddish-brown tree trunks for walls. Both sides of the path are over-grown with large sword ferns, redwood sorrel, and ancient horsetail ferns. There is a stream that follows the path all the way up the mountain.

The heart chakra is green and represents love. I always feel at home in the forest, amongst the greenery of the forest foliage. As I entered the forest and began walking on the gently winding path, I immediately felt relief. As I breathed in the potent oxygen of the forest, my body immediately responded, my muscles, my mind, and my whole being began to relax and let go of the tension that was gripping my body for days.

I did my usual walk, but a shorter version. The shock my brain and body experienced had left me physically exhausted. As I walked, I just focused on my breathing and sense perceptions. I felt the soft earth below my feet, listened to the sound of the flowing stream and the chirping birds. I've always felt that the morning song of the forest birds was pure joy. It was so nice to hear them singing that morning; it reminded me that even thought I felt a great loss, the forest was still filled with wonderment and nothing in my sacred forest had changed. At least one part of life remained the same. It felt like being home, safe, sound, and constant. I felt the cool breeze lovingly caressing my face. I began to relax a little more and to feel engulfed by the sacredness of my familiar forest. I felt the very beginnings of the healing process emerge from the powerful energy of the redwood forest.

The Sun Ray of Eternal Life

Nonphysical consciousness is here with you all the time.

–ABRAHAM HICKS

I walked to my turnaround point at the first bridge. As I was walking back, I was feeling a deep gratitude that Sal, through Gail, had beckoned me to the forest for some much-needed quiet time. I had no idea what was about to happen next.

I was almost back to the trailhead when I got to the small meadow. It is the only place on the path that is not shaded by the redwood trees, and in this section, there are maple trees. I was enjoying the beautiful blends of reds, golds, and browns of the fall foliage and noticing how they were slowly drifting to the ground from the branches of the trees. It was a sunny, crisp fall morning.

I could feel the soothing warmth of the sun rays on my body. As the warmth of the sun rays permeated my body, it further relaxed my muscles. I held my arms up to the sun and with closed eyes looked directly into the sun and took in a deep, slow cleansing breath of pure, fresh forest air. It was precisely at that moment that Sal came in loud and clear. It was almost like his soul rode a sun ray right into my heart!

I have now learned he comes through via light. Whether it is a rainbow, a heart of light in a darkened room, or through the sun itself. He came through like what you might imagine telepathy to be like. It was strong and clear, and I could feel it in my body. It was more like a *knowing* or a *download* than hearing a voice. Later I realized he could not come through until I was alone, and my mind was quiet and relaxed, and that is why he called me to the forest. I was present, just breathing deeply, feeling the warmth of the sun, and hearing the birds welcome the morning in. I walked for a while, relaxed, and stayed present and was also feeling gratitude for the loving embrace of the green forest. This brought me into a state of nonresistance and of allowing. This experience taught me, it is when I am present, relaxed, and feeling gratitude that Sal comes to me.

I could feel Sal, but he was different than how I knew him here on earth. I could feel his specific Sal energy, and yet, there was this wisdom and this vastness to him. The feeling of him is hard to describe in words. When Sal rode that sun ray into my heart that early fall morning, he explained so many crucial things to help me understand the many questions I had. But what was so surprising was that in feeling him in this new vastness, I could also feel my entire being, (my mind, heart, and soul) expand like I have never felt before. I felt us both so vast, and I also knew we had been together as long as forever.

I also felt my father with him. Sal was uncannily like my father, in more ways than what is considered normal. Sal loved all the same things my father had cherished. They even had the same mannerisms; yet, here on earth, they never knew each other. My father passed while I was seven months pregnant with Sal, and of course, Sal is named after my father. I felt myself with him and my father in this formless place of pure, unconditional love and clarity. And I could literally feel my mind expanding and understanding so much more. I didn't retain every bit of what I received, but I did retain the mind-blowing *feeling* of the vast spacious expansion as my true Being. And I did receive so much understanding from Sal's download that helped me immensely. I was not expecting anything like this to happen on my walk in the forest that morning. I did not even know this kind of thing was possible for me.

That beautiful fall day in the meadow of the redwood forest, Sal told me many other personal messages to help me through this tough time. By the time I left the forest I was feeling full of love and compassion. But I was still in shock and still missing the physical Sal so much, I was still heartbroken. Even though I had this amazing experience and I did accept what happened, I still wasn't sure how I could ever live without Sal. I wasn't sure I would ever be able to smile and laugh again.

I wasn't sure anyone could understand what just happened to me; I wasn't even sure I understood! This would take time for me to fully process and absorb the magnitude of this experience. I would need to stay quiet and in presence.

This kind of communication was completely new to me. If I moved to analyzing and doubting, all would be lost. I journaled soon after. I was so grateful for Gail who was present enough in meditation to get the message from Sal. The spirit does work in mysterious ways. And Sal was always a fast learner!

No Death; No Separation

One thing he really made clear is that there simply is no death. He really emphasized this. What we call death is in reality a transition from physical to nonphysical. Or you could say from form to formless. He said it is like walking from inside the house to outside. But also it is like leaving a place of limitation (some of which we ourselves create) to a place of freedom.

He described where he is now as a place of pure positive energy, unconditional love, and clarity. He later takes me to this place (Part II, Chapter Six: A Heavenly Massage).

He told me to never for a moment think I had anything to do with his passing, but that it was something like a contract or a sacred agreement, we both knew he was going to make his transition at an early age.

He told me there is no separation between us, that here on earth, because we are physical, we think we are separate from one another but that simply is not true. In the place where he is now he could see that there is no separation. And for my comfort he stressed that there is no separation between the two of us. That we can continue our relationship with each other and that we are both meant to continuously grow and expand our consciousness. He also told me that he is omnipresent, meaning he can be with many others, and me all at the same time.

He told me that people make too big of a deal out of the death experience. That we need to realize that there is only life and more life—it does not end ever. He explained that the opposite of death is not life—it is birth.

Life has no opposite, life goes on and on, we just change form to have different experiences. I got the feeling that he was telling me, we are life. That life is not something we possess, it is actually what we are. Life is not a thing we possess, and own, those are illusory thoughts. He ended with telling me that he chose not to come back to earth because he can help me and others more from where he is now, than when he was on earth. I have experienced this to be true.

Sacred Contracts

When Sal first came to me that day in the redwood forest, just a few days after he made his transition, it came through loud and clear that we both had agreed to his early departure and that it would help many souls understand their nonphysical nature. Not only through his ability to touch so many people at such a young age but also through the work I am doing now and have been doing for a long time.

I got that we were both uplifters here on earth. He in a way that was out in the world, doing worldly things, and touching so many through his enthusiasm and sheer joy of life. I thought of how he touched everyone he met with his lovable personality, charisma, and sincerity. His days in high school, dedicated to sports, his interest in music, and all the part-time and volunteer jobs he held through high school and college gave him access to hundreds of people.

I, on the other hand, uplift people by teaching meditation and yoga, taking wellness classes, and leading hikes and spiritual retreats. I work with small groups in my garden studio, named The Sacred Garden. I have a spiritually advance group of students, and real transformation happens in The Sacred Garden. I feel one of the best ways to teach is by example; I do my best to live by what I teach. And I teach what I most want to learn. Also, most of my students are healers and teachers themselves. In our own very different ways, Sal and I were both doing the same thing. We were helping people to feel good and live a purposeful life.

Through Sal's transition many of his young friends have told me that they never thought about spirituality until Sal passed. He has given them signs that he is not gone. They look at life differently now and many have come to me and asked me how I've been able to handle this loss so well. In a way, Sal and I are now working together to awaken people to knowing they are timeless, eternal, and connected. That there is more to this world than we can see, hear, touch, smell, and feel with our five senses. That there is an underlying Oneness that transcends all physicality. In writing this book, I feel Sal's guidance inspiring my writing.

Validation

Sal and the universe have this wonderful way of giving me validation for the incredible signs and communications I receive from Sal. I am blessed and grateful that these validations follow many of the messages I get from Sal. Several months after Sal told me about the agreement between us, the sacred contract described above when I was in the forest, just days after he passed, I had a lucid dream, meaning I was conscious in the dream. In the dream it was Sal and I discussing this very idea of being together as mother and son, having a relationship with lots of love and no drama, and also agreeing to his early departure for the good of all and for spiritual growth. In the dream we were like two friends, not mother and son. We are formless, we are beings of light but very real and connected. It started off as a normal dream, but at a certain point, I became conscious in the dream. I needed to have the dream be lucid for a full understanding of our sacred contract. This dream served as validation for the message I received from Sal in the forest.

Sal comes through the cell phone; More Validation on the message in the forest

(Journal Notes summarized)

Friday, December 20, 2013

Sal came to me in the forest, two days after he made his transition. Several weeks after Sal's message in the forest, I began to doubt what I heard and wondered if I had somehow imagined it, even though miracles were occurring all around me and others, from Sal. However, the skeptical mind still needed more validation. I awoke in the middle of the night and questioned myself. I asked Sal for some validation. I had my iphone on my bedside table; I reached for it and put on YouTube. I closed my eyes and randomly scrolled up and down and then tapped the screen. What came up was unbelievable! An Abraham Hicks video. Abraham is a spiritual teacher who answers people's questions. The question was from a woman who lost her son in an automobile accident one month ago! Wow, what are the chances that a mother who lost her son in a vehicle accident would come on and it also had been only a month? Almost identical circumstances I thought, but it got even more synchronistic. Almost everything that Sal told me that day in the forest, Abraham told this woman, minus the more personal information Sal gave me that just pertained to our specific circumstances.

The YouTube audio was thirteen minutes long. Abraham emphasized that there is no death, just like Sal did. Abraham told this mother that her son did not suffer and is near her most of the time. Sal also told me that he did not suffer. That when one dies they actually do not suffer. We suffer more on earth than we do when we make our transition. That death is just a transition from physical to nonphysical, almost like walking from inside to outside. Sal actually gave me that same analogy! The mother said that she had to be in the vortex to reach her son. The vortex is a place of unconditional love. Sal did not use the word vortex, but he took me where he was and it was clearly a place of unconditional love. A place where the love is so strong, tears are streaming down your face. They are tears of pure bliss, you might even say, tears of holy water. There were many other similarities, but those were the most basic and profound messages. And then more validation from the message in the forest came a few years later on Mother's Day.

Another validation of the message in the forest
(Journal Notes revised and summarized).

Sunday, May 14, 2017

This same YouTube audio that I came across a month after Sal's transition in late December 2013 and was a precious gift of validation for all that Sal had told me about life and death in the forest, came to me again on Mother's Day in 2017. It showed up on my email out of nowhere. On Mother's Day morning I had an unusual urge to check my emails as soon as I woke up. I normally do not do this. I wait until after my morning practice and shower to check my emails, especially on a Sunday morning. But I gave in to the urge to check my email and the thirteen-minute recording from Abraham Hicks was sent to me in a random email by YouTube. The only thing on the email was this recording from YouTube. I needed to be reminded of this important message that Sal had told me in the forest and I needed to remember all these important truths. At this point in my life I was dealing with extremely difficult challenges, based on pure survival and it was so easy to fall into fear and egoic thinking.

It was an important sign from Sal to remind me of what was truly important. It was time to remember this important message. And it was a sign from Sal saying Happy Mother's Day, I'm always here for you.

Life Is Good

One of the most important things Sal told me that day in the forest was that instead of thinking that my life will never be good again, I needed to trust that life will unfold in ways I never thought possible. That life would become more adventurous in ways that would be revealed to me. That there was a possibility for me to live with more peace, love, and joy than I had ever known. He told me he would always be with me and that our love, which was already so strong, would continue to grow as would our relationship.

At that time it was very hard for me to believe that my life would ever be good again after losing the physical Sal, let alone, better. However, I now understand what he meant by that and why he gave me that message only two days after he made his exit here on earth. If this message that life was going to evolve to higher plateaus would not have been validated through the iphone (YouTube) or computer (email) on two different occasions shortly after the message in the forest, I would have thought I had misunderstood. At the time Sal passed, most of the aspects of my life were flowing in a good, positive way. My marriage was strained, but everything else was doing well. So how could it get better now that I lost my son who loved me with such intensity and who I loved back with as much intensity? How could it possibly be better here on earth to live a life without the physical Sal? Especially with Arthur, Sal's younger brother, closing down and carrying a heavy burden of pain in his heart.

The reason life has transcended is that when something so horrendous happens, such as losing a child, there is always an opportunity, an open door, to walk through that will take you to a new level of consciousness, a deeper understanding of the meaning of life. I accepted the invitation to experience living in a place of compassion, unshakable inner peace, and love. Loss and adversity seem to open this door, and it is our choice to walk through it, or not.

Through the loss of Sal, I have been forced or highly motivated to stay connected with spirit, so I can feel Sal. In feeling Sal and dwelling more and more in the high vibrations of love and gratitude, I have learned to have an adventurous and playful vibrational relationship with him. And to understand that this life is but a blink of an eye in eternity. And that we are here on earth to awaken, to realize our true Self, and to live with joy.

When you examine the lives of the most influential people who have ever walked among us, you discover one thread that winds through them all. They have been aligned first with their spiritual nature and only then with their physical selves.

–Albert Einstein

You do not need to have a loss to align with Source. My point here is that you use whatever has been your challenge in life to bring you to a higher awareness of consciousness, to a deeper understanding of life, to awaken. All of us have challenges if we have lived here on earth long enough.

During a crisis in our lives, we really have two choices—love or fear. Love will awaken and fear will bring suffering.

Life Is the Guru

With everything that has happened to you, you can either feel sorry for yourself or treat what has happened as a gift. Everything is either an opportunity to grow or an obstacle to keep you from growing. You get to choose.

—Dr. Wayne W. Dyer, PhD, Author, Lecturer

I have had many wonderful spiritual teachers in my life, but I think most would agree that our most obvious teacher is life itself. Life presents to us what we most need to learn, what we have drawn to ourselves, and what we are capable of learning. When we pay close attention to what happens and develop a positive mindset in which to acquire the wisdom from the challenges life presents, we grow and expand. We awaken little by little; life is a process of waking up to Self realization.

I found that when we are asking for big things in life, we get big challenges. And the truth is we are all here for growth and expansion. So later I realized the connection of my intention to awaken and the many big life lessons that were in store for me on this accelerated path. However, I am not stating here that Sal passed because I asked for growth. There is so much our small human minds cannot understand, but there is a trusting that all is in divine order and happening for the highest good of all. When I notice a sequence of events, like my yearning for a deeper understanding and the many challenges I have been presented with in life.

A quote from Eckhart Tolle comes to mind:

True freedom and the end of suffering is living in such a way as if you had completely chosen whatever you feel or experience.

I'm not saying that you or I would ever choose anything like illness or a loss, but to be open to the possibility that our soul chooses growth and growth comes many times in adversity. And simply *feeling* like there might be a possibility that we somehow attracted this for reasons unbeknown to us, empowers us, rather than putting us in the story as a helpless victim.

At the end of the year on my birthday, which is in December, I journal of the occurrences of the entire year. I started this practice long ago when writing daily had become impossible in my busy life. I also write down my goals and an intention word for the upcoming year. For the past five years before Sal passed, all my goals dissolved and I only had one intention: To awaken, to realize down to my soul who I really am.

I had been asking for alignment with Source in a big way, and when Sal made his transition into the realm of pure, unconditional love, it led me, in a very strong way, to follow him into that place where nothing else seems to matter but living in love and peace. The more I moved into this place of a higher vibration, the more my life transformed for the better. I was led by my love for Sal as my guiding star into alignment with the greater part of me.

What our souls need and what we, as human beings think we need is not always the same. But if we can recognize that maybe our soul chose those difficult people and situations in our lives, for growth, then perhaps we can live in a place of empowerment and freedom rather than victim-hood. If we realize that our soul may have a different agenda for our lives, then we do, we can use these challenges for growth. And as we live a sur-rendered life, we naturally become aligned with our Source.

When we are living from this higher place, life flows with ease, and we can become one with life. Realizing that life is the dancer and we are the dance, the spacious awareness that holds the space for life to flow, to dance. When this realization occurs, challenges do not disappear from our lives, but we do not take life so seriously because we are aware of the bigger pic-ture. And we then have the ability to respond to life rather than react to life, such knee-jerk reacting without conscious awareness can definitely cause more drama. Responding intelligently while staying present and accepting what is, are tools that can make this life on earth much more enjoyable. The freedom to choose how we respond in life, is the ultimate freedom that can never be taken from us.

Everything can be taken from a man but one thing: the last of the human freedoms—to choose one's attitude in any given set of circumstances, to choose one's own way.

–VIKTOR FRANKL, AUTHOR—MAN'S SEARCH FOR MEANING

PART II:

CONNECTION
AND SIGNS

CHAPTER THREE:

Connect with Your Loved Ones

Some Beliefs Can Be Obstacles

I wish I could show you when you are lonely in the darkness,
the astonishing light of your own being.

—HAFIZ, POET

Buddha narrated a parable which shows that if you hold on to one idea, one belief and consider it to be "the truth," then you may miss the chance to know the truth. If you are trapped in doctrines and are in a state of resistance, you lose any chance of your own direct experience of the truth.

This parable of the Buddha is told by Thich Nhat Hanh:

"A young tradesman came home and saw that his house had been robbed and burned by bandits. Right outside what was left of the house, there was a small charred body. He thought the body belonged to his little boy. He did not know that his child was still alive. He did not know that after having burned the house, the bandits had taken the little boy away with them. In his confusion, the tradesman believed the body he saw was his son. So he cried in grief and began the cremation ceremony.

The man loved his little boy so much, he carried the ashes with him at all times. One night the boy escaped from the robbers. At two in the morning the little boy came to the new house his father had built. He knocked excitedly on the door. The father called out as he wept, still holding on to the ashes. "Who is there?"

"It's me, your son!" The boy answered through the door. "You naughty person, you are not my boy. My child died three months ago, I have his ashes with me right now here." The little boy continued to beat on the door and cried and cried. He begged over and over to come in, but his father continued to refuse him entry. The man held firm to the notion that his little boy was already dead and that this other child was some heartless person who had come to torment him. Finally the boy left and the father lost his son forever."

When we have stubborn old beliefs about death that we have never questioned, but simply accepted because we have had them for so long, they become imbedded in our psyche. Beliefs are just thoughts we keep thinking over and over until they become etched in our minds. When this happens, it denies us fresh, new perspectives of life. We don't need to believe what someone else tells us about death, whether it is positive or negative. But we do need to be open enough to allow ourselves to have our own direct experiences in life, instead of believing old, rigid doctrines that someone else has planted in our heads years ago. It would be more desirable to have our own direct experience. For this we need to be open, nonjudgmental, and independent thinkers.

Why not try giving your deceased loved ones a chance to show you they are near? Be relaxed, open, and childlike and most importantly be aware, be present. Be quiet and still and see what happens. Appreciate the signs you do get, be at ease, and let life flow, as it was meant to be. When I let my guard down and let go of fear and judgment, I notice that life is friendly toward me. Some refer to this as living a surrendered life. A surrendered life is living life in acceptance of what is. More on this in in Part III on acceptance.

In this section of the book, I invite you to let go of those old, limited beliefs and doctrines and be open to the infinite possibilities that tug at your heart and soul.

Signs Can Strengthen Our Connection

Intuition is the voice of the nonphysical world

–GARY ZUKAV, AUTHOR

Let's entertain the idea that anyone can connect with their loved ones who have left their physical bodies here on earth. I have had hundreds of signs from Sal, too many to write off as coincidences and too solid to be imagination. Besides all of the incredible signs, I have also received validation to show that the communication and the sign were real. I alone do not receive signs from Sal, but many of our family members and friends also do. Even people who did not know him while he was here on earth, but were connected with me, have received his signs.

As I share my experiences of the signs from Sal with all kinds of different people from all parts of the world, almost every one of them has a similar story to share with me of a loved one who has made their transition into the formless realm, and have given them a sign that they are near. Most of these signs are quite obvious to the recipient that the sign was meant for them. They also have a strong intuitive feeling in their heart that this sign is from their loved one. Trust your intuitive heart; it is inherently wise.

To receive these signs, it may help if you have a desire to receive these and if you hold in your mind that this is possible. It helps if you have a clear and calm mind. It takes what I call, having you eyes wide open. What I mean by that is that our loved ones are often trying to reach us, especially right after they made their transition or on their birthdays or on other significant dates. Sal always give me surprising signs on Mother's Day and when I have events in his honor, usually on the exact date of his birthday.

We need to have an open and acute awareness, so we can notice these playful signs and intuitive feelings. Knowing and trusting the subtle voice of intuition is needed. Our formless loved ones want us to know they are still here and they are interested in playing with us and connecting with us. They want us to know they are happy and in a good place. When we see a heart of light on our wall in a dark room, or their birthday at a perfect time, we need to acknowledge it and appreciate it. In the section on signs you will read about the many ways your loved ones may try to reach you. So, much of the time we want to believe that the rainbow or the butterfly was a sign from our loved one, but we feel we are just being silly or ridiculously hopeful. That judgmental voice in the head leads us away from our own joy and our own intuitive knowing, and the loud voice of doubt surfaces and wins over our own quiet intuition. We are afraid, so we doubt. We are afraid to take a chance and go deeper into our own intuitive guidance system. We are afraid of what others might think of us, or afraid to believe or have faith. Remember the voice of our intuition is quiet and the inner critic and doubter are loud. Be still and listen for the truth. The truth is always available, we just need to get still, be quiet, and listen within.

Why do so many of us let go of the signs we have received from our passed loved ones? Why do we forget about the heartfelt emotions we get when we first see the sign and instinctively know that this sign was meant for us? As time passes and we get busy with our lives, we forget. Why do we not realize that if we so choose, we can continue to feel our connection with that loved one? Why do we let these signs fade with time? Perhaps it is because our world does not accept these truths or maybe because we have never been taught how to stay connected with our deceased loved ones or even told this is possible. Maybe it is because we don't practice presence or make time in our life to be alone in meditation or contemplation. Maybe it is because we do not realize we are timeless, eternal spiritual beings having a human experience. Possibly, negativity is slowing taking us over and hope is fading for us.

The limited mind may say, "Oh, that was just your imagination or a coincidence." This is why it is so important to take photos and journal as soon as possible after receiving the sign. In the very beginning I was getting so many signs that I was just causally enjoying them, but I was not taking photos or journaling them. But, I quickly learned to journal these signs as soon as they happened. I have three journals full of signs from Sal. The way to increase the signs from your loved ones is to acknowledge them and know they are real, to enjoy them, and allow yourself to feel gratitude for them. It feels good to feel gratitude and it is fun, but best of all, there is a universal law that occurs when we feel gratitude. It goes like this: the more grateful we are, the more abundance appears in our life. Wherever we put our attention is where our energy goes. So when we feel appreciation for the fun signs from our passed loved ones, the more they come.

There is no need to lament when our passed loved ones are not sending signs, rather trust and have faith that nonphysical is part of your reality. In fact, the larger part of you is nonphysical. It is enough to feel love for them and feel love from them. Signs are not necessary, they are just fun.

I now take photos of the signs and share them through emails with my students, family, and friends. I receive many texts and emails from Sal's family and friends with photos of rainbows or other signs that they know came from Sal. I feel these signs are meant to be shared, because it lets everyone in on the fun and most importantly it demonstrates that life goes on after the death of the body.

Many of us started posting many of these miraculous signs on social media as well. It is always fun to get the responses and support from friends and family. As more people share these experiences, they actually become more widely spread and even expected. This is part of consciousness expanding and the thinning of the veil between the physical and nonphysical. Our minds have become more open to infinite possibilities and our long-held resistance is beginning to melt.

Evolving Into Wholeness

One of the main reasons we are now becoming aware that we can keep our connection with passed loved ones is that we are evolving as conscious human beings and becoming more multisensory. Multisensory or six sensory, as it is sometimes called, refers to our sense of intuition, our sense of the nonphysical. Our sense of perception beyond our five physical senses of what we can see, hear, touch, smell, and taste. Intuition is defined as a direct perception of truth and an instinctive knowing without reason.

As you become more intuitive, you begin to see yourself as a soul first and a personality second. You begin to experience yourself as more than your physical body, your repetitive thoughts, and more than your analytical mind. You begin to realize that the circumstances around you have meaning and are actually there to give you the opportunity for spiritual growth. You realize that life is designed for our evolution and expansion. Your life begins to fill with synchronic events and this becomes the norm for you.

As human beings evolve, this connection to loved ones who have made their transition is growing. Sal, through my own intuition, has led me to several books that address this very topic—the possibility of staying connected with our passed loved ones.

Even though there are people who cling to the old, dying reality, a new one is being born, and rich, fulfilling relationships between the living and what we call the dead are at the center of it."

–WHITLEY AND ANNE STRIEBER, AUTHORS—
THE AFTERLIFE REVOLUTION.

Human beings are becoming more whole as they evolve; we are aware of not only our physical body, mind, and the five senses but also our sixth sense, our intuition, and our nonphysical nature. You can see this quality in the young ones; they use their inner guidance system and intuition to play on iPads at the age of only two years old. They do not need the instruction manual.

When we ignore our heartfelt sense of pure awareness, of the nonphysical realm, we are not whole. It is natural for human beings to be aware of feelings and perceptions, to be intuitive. If we lived life by having to have proof of everything, by having to see it first, we would be stifled and not allow the development of our intuitive abilities to grow and develop. This is an incredible handicap, and would lead us to very sheltered lives, living in a place of fear, instead of trust, knowing, and faith. Many who live this way never develop the ability to be comfortable with uncertainty. When you can learn to live life tuned in to your higher intelligence and your intuition, you lead a much more fulfilled and adventurous life. You learn that you have clarity, but sometimes, only on the next baby step you need to take at the moment. You accept that you cannot get the whole picture all at once, and if you trust and follow your inner guidance, you will get what you need at the time that you need it. It is empowering to live life this way, and it is the way we were meant to live. Most of us are not taught this from our parents or our teachers. Those of us who live this way have learned this from life itself or from ancient spiritual teachings. To be whole, we need to live from a place of being multisensory; using and developing all the gifts that were given to live full whole lives; and moving from external ego-based power to authentic spiritual power.

One of my favorite affirmations to use to increase my intuitional abilities is given by Paramahansa Yogananda: *I go forth in perfect faith with the power of omnipresent good to bring me what I need at the time that I need it.*

Feeling Is Enough

I would like to add that many of us get more signs closer to the transition of our loved ones than later on. If you really like the signs, you can ask your loved one to keep them coming. But after so many signs we can probably accept that we really do not need the signs all the time. Once in a while on a special day for either you or your loved one can be enough. The signs help us to develop a strong knowing and we learn to feel their presence with us. Feeling them is what is most important. Once secure in our own guidance system, we don't need constant signs.

This is a personal choice we can all make. It is different for all of us. Just the other day while writing this book, I asked Sal for a sign, just to be playful, and honestly, I never get tired of his signs. Later that afternoon I went for a walk from my apartment. He gave me two very creative signs, which are described in the following section. It warmed my heart and made me smile and laugh out loud.

One mistake I have made in the past, is that I thought I had to let a deceased loved one go. But what is true is that our loved ones can be with us whenever we call them in. You can even say I need you near most of the time. Because time does not exist in the formless realm. Time is a man-made concept. Also, they are omnipresent, they can be in more than one place at the same time. Everything and everyone is made of energy.

Another strange habit energetic particles have is they can be in more than one place at the same time. Called "superposition," electrons and other non-particle particles are capable of being in hundreds of places simultaneously, which is only possible if everything is energy at the most fundamental levels.

–CATE MONTANA, M.A., AUTHOR—THE ILLUSION OF REALITY: THE SCIENTIFIC PROOF THAT EVERYTHING IS ENERGY AND REALITY ISN'T REAL

Develop a Vibrational Relationship

Existence is vibration.

–DR. MASARU EMOTO, MD, AUTHOR

The vibrational relationship is a relationship with someone who is now formless. We can feel their presence, we know what it feels like to be near them. For example, if your loved one was sitting right next to you and you had a blindfold on, could you tell who it was? Would you know if it was your lover or your uncle? Could you *feel* their presence? We all vibrate at different rates. This is true, whether in a physical body or not.

The science of quantum mechanics shows that substance is nothing more than vibration. A simple fact of physics is that we are 99.9% space. What's left is vibrating particles, energy. What appears to be solid is, in actuality, vibrating atoms, each atom with a nucleus and electrons rotating around it. Every substance that looks solid to us is only a nucleus with an endless rotating wave. This is hard for our small human minds to understand, so don't worry, if your logical mind is now spinning, just let it go for now and stay with me.

I love this quote by the Buddha to further explain how existence is vibration. Science is finally catching up with what the Buddha was teaching over two thousand five hundred years ago.

That which can be seen has no form; that which cannot be seen has form.

–The Buddha

My definition for a relationship with a passed loved one is a vibrational relationship. You cannot see them but you can feel them. You can feel their particular vibe. Each human being has their own unique frequency.

Everyone knows what it's like to be with a person who has a positive outlook and an innate enthusiasm for life. You feel uplifted when you are with a person like this.

You notice that you have more energy and feel happy after spending time with this person. And you can also feel their energy when they are with you. You would know that energy anywhere, even if that person was invisible. Then there is the person, who is always negative and unhappy. After spending a little time with this person, you feel drained and you just want to go home, take a nap, and get away from them. And again, you know what that energy feels like, whether or not you can see that person.

Each one of us has the sensory skills necessary to feel the vibrations of others.

This feeling cannot be described in words; you have to experience it for yourself. But before you can get there, you have to be open to the possibility of the existence of nonphysical, and that nonphysical is vibrational and that you too are vibrational and physical. In fact, science has proven that *everything is* energy. To feel another person's vibration, you can learn to develop your intuitive/feeling skills. Being present is one of the best ways to develop your gift of multisensory perception.

A simple way to develop your intuition is by simply sitting in stillness and being aware of all your five senses. You can pick just one of your five senses. Hearing for example: As you walk from the car to grocery store, can you hear the birds singing? In a noisy restaurant can you hear the hum of conversations? Other ways to develop your intuition is through meditation and contemplation. Start guessing, who's going to win the game, who's bluffing in your poker game, and who's knocking on your door?

Begin to notice when the underlying life force is bringing you wonderment. When that beautiful rainbow appears right over your house as you are thinking of your loved one. When you start seeing hearts everywhere, in cloud formations, in leafs, and shells on the beach. Notice these gifts, and the more you do, the more your life transforms into a life you never knew could exist here on earth. Your life will be full of synchrony and you will feel lucky. To others, your life looks magical, as the veil between the form and the formless thins, but this is the way life is meant to be lived.

This is a time of awakening, awakening to knowing we are so much more than our physicality and mind. Even though there is currently so much turmoil in the world around us, if you look deeper you will see an energy emerging beneath the chaos of humans beginning to be more conscious. More people are talking about energy, vibration, meditation, healing the environment, and so forth. More are beginning to be aware of a connection to each other and to a higher intelligence. This can be a time of knowing we are loved, guided, protected, connected, and supported more than we know. Open up to the possibilities of this infinite universe, and let the power of the unseen allow your life to unfold in ways that feel miraculous and alive.

The Key to Connection

Love is always bestowed as a gift—freely, willingly and without expectation.
We don't love to be loved; we love to love.

–LEO BUSCAGLIA, TEACHER, AUTHOR

I found that the key to my connection with Sal is both love and gratitude and staying present. Why? Love, gratitude, and presence are all of a high vibration. I have learned that to connect with Sal I need to be relaxed, present, at ease, and flowing with life. If I am in resistance Sal cannot reach me.

Physics tell us that we are all vibrating molecules of energy. Physics also tells us that like attracts like. Meaning that we are always attracting into our lives similar vibrating molecules of energy. So with Sal now being in a place of pure positive energy and vibrating at a higher level, I have to match that vibration if I want to feel him. So in other words, I need to be in a place of appreciation, love, or presence to feel Sal. Most of the times when

I get signs from him is when I am relaxed and feeling good, not when I am feeling angst or worried. Usually when I am calling to him in one of those states, I do not get a sign or feel him until I am relaxed and not thinking about anything in particular.

Ancient Method of Connection

Ancient yogic wisdom teachings tell us that it is absolutely possible to connect with passed loved ones and that it is also possible to continue our relationship with them. Not just continue our relationship but also allow that relationship to flourish and expand.

Paramahansa Yogananda, one of the first yogi masters who came from India to America in the early 1900s to teach the West the spiritual principles of the East and who wrote the classic, *Autobiography of a Yogi*, explains it this way:

Communicating with souls in the astral world is not a simple accomplishment. It is an ancient science secretly guarded by nature: If we love purely and unselfishly, and develop spiritually, we can learn the secret science of maintaining a link with our loved ones after death.

I learned from Paramahansa Yogananda how to connect with passed loved ones by reading his little booklet, *Where Are Our Departed Loved Ones?* I not only learned an effective technique but I also experienced the absolute truth of this teaching from direct experience, the first time I practiced this technique.

In his own words:

To send your thoughts to loved ones who have passed on, sit quietly in your room and meditate upon God. When you feel His peace within you, concentrate deeply at the Christ center, the center of will at the point between the eyebrows, and broadcast your love to those dear ones who are gone. Visualize at the Christ center the person you wish to contact. Send to that soul your vibrations of love, and of strength, and courage. If you do this continuously, and if you do not lose the intensity of your interest of that loved one, that soul will definitely receive your vibrations.

−PARAMAHANSA YOGANANDA, SELF-REALIZED SAGE

The first time I practiced this was in India in 2005. I was homeschooling my younger son, Arthur. Arthur was in the seventh grade and he was studying world history. India was not even mentioned in the seventh-grade text book, so I made it a point to study India on our own. And what better way to learn about this magnificent country than to visit it. I was so grateful I had saved up enough mileage points to make this trip a possibility for Arthur and me. I knew this trip would forever change his view of the world.

My mother had just passed away about two weeks before we left for India. I was worried about my mother, because she was in a very depressed state of mind when she made her transition. I had picked up this booklet in a store in Gurgaon, India, called *The Tree of Life*. Arthur and I were on a tour with a group from Ananda Church, a spiritual center of Self-Realization. We were staying in a hotel in Gurgaon, a suburb of New Delhi. I was anxious to read the book. We were on the top floor of the hotel at the pool. Arthur and some other boys were swimming and playing around while I was enjoying the sun and reading the book. When I got to the part on this technique, I decided to practice it. I closed my eyes and faced the sun and saw my mother at the point between my eyebrows, also known as the third eye, spiritual eye, Christ center, brow center, or single eye. The spiritual eye is at the sixth chakra. It is where one can connect with super-consciousness, intuition, and wisdom. Jesus also spoke of the spiritual eye.

When thine eye is single, thy whole body also is full of light...
Take heed therefore that the light which is in thee be not darkness

−LUKE 11:34-35.

As I visualized my mother at the spiritual eye, I saw her surrounded by a luminous white light. I sent her love and thoughts of well-being. I did this intensely, but for only a few minutes, as I wanted to keep an eye on my son and the other boys. I thought of this, as practice and decided I would do this for a much longer time in my morning meditation the next day. That night something completely unexpected happened.

Arthur and I had a room with two twin beds. That night I slept well. In the wee hours of the morning, while it was still dark outside, I had a dream of my deceased mother and father coming to me. It started as a very vivid dream, but then the most unbelievable thing happened: I opened my eyes and I could literally see both my mother and father standing right in front of me, at the foot of the bed. They were both glowing with love for me and for each other. They looked radiant and they were physical! They both looked like they did when I was a child. They looked young and happy and vibrant. In the dream, my father who was always very optimistic, appeared first and told me he was with my mother and she was doing well. He was helping her to heal and adjust to the formless realm. Then my mother appeared as she came out from behind my father and assured me that she was fine. At that point the dream had become lucid and I open my eyes to see both of them standing right at the foot of my bed, as real as ever. After approximately forty-five seconds of eyes wide open, enjoying my mom and dad in the physical, I reached my arm out to Arthur but the beds were too far away, I wanted him to see what I was seeing. But, both my mother and father had vanished, before I could wake him.

I later learned this is called a visitation and is quite rare, but I have met others who have also experienced this. Besides being shown that our loved ones are near to us, I also learned an important lesson on meditation and the power of the mind. I learned that in meditation, it is not about how long you sit in meditation, but rather, the intensity of concentration you hold in meditation, which is key. We sometimes think we need to sit for hours in meditation to receive insights and truth. But if you sit for hours with a wondering mind, in the East, they call this monkey mind, you will not get the insights. However, if you sit for a short time with a calm, focused mind, you will receive insights and the many benefits of meditation. This is not to say, do not meditate if you have monkey mind, because we all do. It is in the practice that we learn to calm the mind. So maybe you have to go through forty minutes of monkey mind to get five minutes of true connection with God/Source. That is worth it! Besides, the studies show that practicing meditation has many benefits, even if you are not in the "zone" at all times. My point here is to make the effort of intense concentration, to stay present. Be alert and still in meditation; do not just see your practice as a chance to sit and space out. More on meditation in Part III.

How I Connect

My near death experience, showed me that the death of the body and the brain are not the end of consciousness, that human experience continues beyond the grave.

–Eben Alexander MD, Author

It is very important to realize that our formless loved ones are very near. They are happy to connect with us. It is our choice to feel them and connect with them through prayer, meditation, or just talking to them. They hear us; they are usually in a more loving place, and they are watching over us. From my own experience, there is no doubt in my mind that this is true.

When you get a sign, cherish it. . Allow yourself to smile and laugh and play with them and ignore the fact that you can't see or hear them. As you read all the signs Sal has given me and others, it will give you an idea of what I am talking about. You will see how Sal and I have a playful relationship and how he helps me with finding items I have misplaced and gives me guidance on more important issues. They still enjoy your love and prayers. They are still family with you or still friends with you. They still care about you and your life. They love you more now than ever. And the love can grow and flourish if you keep them close to your heart.

I personally connect with Sal by using the same technique as mentioned above. I close my eyes and lift my inner gaze upward at the point between the eyebrows. As previously mentioned this point between the eyebrows is the positive pole of the sixth chakra and is where one can connect with the Infinite Intelligence and loved ones.

When I connect with Sal using this technique, the gaze is a gentle upward and outward gaze. Do not go crossed eye, if you feel tension, you are going cross-eyed. If you feel a shift to a heighten state of consciousness or an uplifted feeling, you are in the right place; it is subtle, but real. Your eyes get stronger as you practice this. At first it takes more effort, and it might strain your eyes a bit to keep them uplifted. Once I'm centered at the spiritual eye, I visualize Sal's face at the spiritual eye and I focus in on his eyes. I make my connection mainly to his eyes, which many have said, are the windows to the soul. After my profound personal experience with this practice, I would say, the above statement, the eyes are the window to the soul, is correct. At the spiritual eye I see Sal surrounded by a beautiful divine white light and see him perfect, radiant, and full of love. I feel my love for him begin to expand and grow, and I send it out to him. I know feeling the intensity of the love between us and sending it out to him is the key to reaching him.

When I practice this, I feel Sal's love flowing right back to me. It is not necessary for you to feel this, but it feels wonderful and may enhance the connection. Just relax, focus on their eyes, and send them your love. It is that simple, but it takes concentration and steadiness. They will feel your love and your connection to them. Don't worry about getting a sign; the connection is what is important. Trust that your love has been felt by them and then be open to receiving their love flowing back to you. It may come as a dream, a sign, or just a feeling. When you practice this technique, you are developing your intuition and moving into wholeness. Know that there is no separation between you and your loved one. Remember that nothing real can be threatened. Know that your love is real and can never be destroyed, ever!

The mindset that is imperative to connection is to realize that you now have a vibrational relationship with your loved one. They have not gone anywhere, only their body is gone. When you think about it, the truth is, all of our children grow up and that infant, toddler, little child, or teen-ager is no longer here on earth. When you look at your adult children's baby photos there is no reflection of the babies they once were. In a way you can say that those babies are deceased, yet most of us do not mourn this loss. In much the same way, the twenty-four-year-old Sal is gone, but his true essence is here—it is just formless. Here on earth it is an accepted fact that while we are here, we will continuously change and grow in body and mind. We learn all through our lives and our bodies continuously age and change all through our lives. In the same way, your relationship with that nonphysical loved one is evolving over the years and neither one of you are the same now, as you were when they passed. Whether we are in form or formless, we are still expanding and our relationships are always growing in depth, if we so choose.

Sal is not frozen as that twenty-four-year-old who left the planet in 2013 nor is he the thirty-one-year-old he would be today if he had not left. He is now a formless spiritual being. He is wise and loving as ever and is my constant companion. He is different than he was in form. He has a bird's eye view of life now and a different perspective than he did when he was on earth as a twenty-four-year-old man. He knows so much more than he did while on earth. Do not lock your loved ones into the person they were when they exited this planet. Allow them to be who they are now. Do not look for them where they are not, in the house in their favorite chair or at the graveyard, they are nearer than near and still very interested in you and your life. Sal and I are more like best friends now than mother and son. The form of our relationship has changed, but we still have an irreplaceable relationship that is ever-growing and ever-expanding to new heights of fun, love, and connection.

It is hard to hear this and it seems unfair, but when we miss them and become depressed, we can't feel them or reach them. They cannot reach us through our intense suffering and grief. Grief is on a very different vibration than love, where they now reside. Grief is probably the most difficult emotion we can feel as humans; use it for growth and awakening. Breathe deep and observe it in your body and mind, do not judge yourself, and just be aware of what you are feeling. Realize that this grief is NOT who you are, it is temporary, and you can find your way out. However, do not push yourself out of grief, rather just let it stay until it is ready to leave. That is why it is important to just observe it when it comes; the awareness that this grief is not your true nature is enough to let it pass when appropriate for you.

The key here is to stay in the present with your life and your loved one, and then gratitude and love will naturally follow. Do not dwell in the past; the decreased are not there. What I learned to do almost immediately after Sal made his transition was when I looked into the eyes of Sal in a photo or in my mind's eye, I would immediately feel our intense love for one another and as soon as I felt the love, I would go straight to feeling gratitude. I would say, *I love you so much, thank you for being my son here on earth, for almost twenty-five years.* This amazing soul could have picked anyone for his mother, but he picked me. That is something to be grateful for! And then I feel high from the love and gratitude and move on with my day, reveling in the high vibrations of love and appreciation. These two emotions are the highest feelings we as humans can experience. It just doesn't get better than love and gratitude.

Sal's portrait hangs in our home at the bottom of our staircase, I have an electric candle on a little shelf just below the portrait. It is glowing continuously and never goes out. When I come down the stairs every morning, I simply say, I *love you, thank you.* And I feel great, feeling the love and gratitude. I do not think, why did you go so early? It is wrong for children to die before their parents, why did this happen to me? No, those are the voices of the storyteller, also known as the inner critic and the doubter. Please do not go there, it only causes pain and suffering, rather, stay present, let the past go, it's gone anyway, and if you think about it, all we ever have in life is this moment. And this moment is the best place to be, always.

If you feel sad by looking at a photo of the past, just observe your emotions of sadness and know that the higher part of you can feel the love, but right now that lower part is dominating your thoughts and emotions, observe it, feel it, and do not identify with it. Be kind and gentle with yourself; everyone will feel low at times. But, you can recognize it for what it is; let it be and it will pass.

It is important to remember that sometimes we just need to cry; we are human and we miss their physicality, their bodies, their humanness. I look at crying as a great cleanser and sometimes we need it and we sometimes feel better afterwards. However, as I stay in love in gratitude, I find I rarely need a "good cry." To feel excruciating pain because you miss someone so much and love them so much is really a beautiful thing. When this happens to me, I am grateful that I have these strong feelings. It means I loved and lived fully. Not everyone knows this intense love, and if you do, you are blessed.

This technique is a powerful and helpful practice to connect with your loved ones; however, it is not always necessary to do this. We can just allow our own knowing that we are always connected and have trust, faith, and fun with this knowing. Now I simply connect with Sal by just feeling him or talking to him in my mind.

Sal, My Bridge to Heaven

When great loss happens – deaths close to you or your own approaching death - this is an opportunity for stepping completely out of identification with form and realizing the essence of who you are, or that the essence of anyone who is suffering or dying is beyond death.

−Eckhart Tolle, Author and Teacher

As I mentioned above, Sal is not a twenty-four-year-old individual now. He is now in his essence, yet he does have that same Sal energy. Why? Because he was always his essence even while here on earth and so are we. Do you know that part of you that you felt as a child, a teenager, or a young adult, and now, that part of you that was always with you for as long as you can remember? That part of you that is consistent and has observed your life from the background. That is you! That is the witness consciousness, your true essence, your soul—it has been called many things. It is the underlying intelligence that sustains the physical vehicle; it is invisible. It holds the atoms and molecules together so the body can function. But this underlying intelligence, your being, is an aspect of the Universal Intelligence. It can be no other way. You can't see it or look at it under a microscope. When this aspect of the Universal Intelligence leaves the body, the body dies.

The body was never your loved one. Our body is just the costume of our being while in this physical realm called earth. Most of what is essential—love, gratitude, thoughts, emotions, consciousness—is invisible. So as human beings on earth we are mostly invisible. Think of it this way: the being that was underlying the body, allowing it to function, is still here. The body is gone, after the physical death, but not the consciousness/being of that loved one. You may have identified your loved one with that particular body (costume) they were wearing at the time of death. And you freeze them in that body and that age when they died. But their essence is now soaring out of that dead body that is no longer serving them as they make their transition. Their soul has chosen to leave that body.

As I have learned to tap into Sal in the nonphysical, I am actually learning to tap into my own true essence, as well. I feel it awakens me to my true essence as I connect with Sal. When I connect with Sal on a soul level, we are both felt as beings of light more than mother and son. We are both perfectly whole and balanced between feminine and masculine energy.

This is a skill to be practiced, but it is actually easy, because it is enjoyable. Every morning I start my day off with first connecting to the Infinite Intelligence and Sal in meditation. I actually connect to other passed loved ones as well. After I connect in the beginning of my morning meditation, I do my best to stay in mindful, present moment living throughout the day. This is a practice that takes focus and awareness. I have not mastered it by any means, but I have made progress. I know that when I call on Sal during the day for help, he is there. What I have experienced is that in my connection with him, I am fully present with the greater part of my Self, what some refer to as Infinite Intelligence, Source, Consciousness, or God. I realize that Sal is a bridge for me to do that. It is through our human love for each other that we are led to the Oneness underlying all human life. The Oneness that connects us all; the Oneness that we are all a part of—it is greater than all the parts. We are all droplets of the One Life that permeates our entire being and everything else. Our gateway to this heartfelt Oneness is pure, unconditional love. A mother's love for her children is often the most pure, unconditional love that exits on earth.

Quantum physics thus revels a basic oneness of the universe.

–ERWIN SCHRÖDINGER, NOBEL PRIZE–WINNING
AUSTRIAN-IRISH PHYSICIST

Feeling connected to each other and to the Oneness, allows life to feel vibrant and alive. I feel that no matter what the outside conditions are, I am living from a place of unconditional love because I am finding it from within and not from life's circumstances. I feel more grounded in my being than ever before. I feel more awake in the game of life. And I know this awakening business is a process for most of us. I do not feel this all the time.

We are meant to enjoy life, to live with joy and ease. If you do not strive for that, you are missing the meaning of your highest purpose. Your highest purpose is to know who you truly are. And when you realize that, it becomes natural for you to live a life of joy, service, and peace.

I'm not saying I never feel sad or low or I do not miss Sal or other loved ones. I'm not saying I never feel fear. I am human and I sometimes feel sad and fear, and if I need to cry, I allow myself to cry. But it always feels like a deep cleanse. And it isn't long before I feel inspired and filled with gratitude and love again. Through my intense love for Sal and from his intense love for me, I have found my way home. He has truly been my bridge to the Divine, to the way home, my bridge from earth to heaven. I have learned that heaven is a state of mind and not necessarily a specific place. When we experience the spaciousness of unconditional love and peace within us, that is heaven. That is a state of consciousness that is felt as deep peace and can rarely be shaken once you are fully immersed in it.

Signs from Sal

Sal has sent so many signs since his transition; however, I picked only a handful of different ways he has shown me he is here, in the hopes that it will help you to notice all the crazy and fun ways our loved ones attempt to reach us. It is not always rainbows, butterflies, and humming birds. Those and some others are universal, but I have witnessed some truly original signs. And I feel there is no end to the many creative ways our loved ones reach out to us.

I would also like to add here that not all souls choose to give signs the way Sal does. On earth he worked hard at accomplishing whatever it was that he was trying to do. He stuck with things until he could do it and do it well. This trait made him the A student, the star athlete, and so on. Could it be that we carry our traits with us to the other side? He gets better and better with giving signs in new ways. But this is unusual, so just notice all the different and surprising ways signs can be delivered to us and enjoy the humor and creativity.

CHAPTER FOUR:

Sal Plays With Light

The Magic of Light

The law of miracles is operable by any man who has realized that the essence of creation is LIGHT.

−Paramahansa Yogananda, Author, Teacher, Sage

Some of these signs from Sal were written in my journals, immediately after receiving the sign. They have been revised to fit the structure of this book.

The first way that Sal started showing us that he was here with us was through rainbows. Many of us who were devastated by the death of Sal were getting healing rainbow signs just a few days after he passed. These rainbows that came with *healing* qualities were much needed during the hard times after losing a young person so unexpectedly.

Sal seems to play with light and make astonishing things happen. Before Sal passed I had already scheduled to start teaching the *Autobiography of a Yogi* by Paramahansa Yogananda, in my spiritual teachings class. Sal passed at the end of November and I was scheduled to start teaching the book in January, just five weeks after Sal passed. I did stick with my schedule and started teaching these yogic principles at the start of the new year. As I looked back now, I see that teaching that book at that particular time was perfect for me to be open to all the miracles that were occurring in my life in relation to Sal's passing. There appeared to be a divine order or synchronicity taking place.

If ever there was a book to help you think outside the box, it is the *Autobiography of a Yogi*. There are forty-eight chapters and we studied one chapter a week so it took us almost the entire year after Sal passed. The *Autobiography of a Yogi* is the *only* book that Steve Jobs had on his iPhone, and it was given out to everyone who attended his memorial service. And Steve Jobs definitely thought "outside the box."

I had been a meditator for many years and so my intuition was growing stronger as a benefit of meditation. But after the months that Sal passed, the veil between this physical earth world and the formless realm became thinner. So through my studying and teaching of the *Autobiography of a Yogi*, I developed a better understanding of what was happening. I had read this book several times before over the past thirty years, but it had been a long time since I last read it and I had never read it so deeply and slowly. Chapter 30, "The Law of Miracles," really gave me insight into how Sal was working with light. Even though the book was written almost sixty years ago, Paramahansa Yogananda was on top of the science behind miracles from the available leading-edge scientific discoveries of 1940s and the ancient teachings of the Vedas. It is always nice when I see our contemporary science making discoveries that the ancient sages have been teaching for centuries.

The book states that light is the only thing in is this universe that is stable, and that light has the ability to pass freely through the vacuum of interstellar space. He also talks about how the velocity of light is the only constant in a universe of duality and unstable flux.

Chapter 30 speaks of the quality of light, Yogananda writes:

*Among the trillion mysteries of the cosmos, the most phenomenal is light. Unlike sound waves, whose transmission requires air or other material media, **light** waves pass freely through the vacuum of interstellar space. **Light** remains the most subtle, the freest from material dependence of any natural manifestation. Einstein proves mathematically that the velocity of light is,* *so far as man's finite mind is concerned, the only constant in a universe of unstable flux.*

Eternal Love, Rainbows, and My Yoga Mat

Journal Notes: May 2014

As I was rolling up my yoga mat this morning after my morning practice, there were several beautiful rainbows on it, little rainbows reflecting from some crystals hanging near the window. The morning sun was dazzling the room with twinkling little round rainbows. As previously mentioned, rainbows have come to represent one of the ways Sal's love comes to me and others. As I was rolling up the mat and enjoying the rainbows, I thought for just a moment that I was rolling up the rainbows too, but of course that is a silly thought, because the rainbows were now on the carpet where the mat once was. And I thought what a beautiful analogy to show how love is real and cannot be erased or lost. If you think of the mat as Sal's physical body, which got rolled up on November 25, 2013, and the rainbows as our eternal love, it shows how eternal love is not one bit affected by the mat being rolled up and taken away. And as I have come to learn, light is the one thing in the universe that is not dualistic and it easily passes through different dimensions. The rainbows which are colored light is the perfect analogy to show how nothing real (true unconditional love) can be threatened, or rolled up! Life is always speaking to us; we just need to pay attention!

Rainbow Signs

When Sal first made his transition he began coming to many of us in the form of rainbows. After reading the section above you can understand why it is very common for our formless loved ones to come to us in rainbows and light. In the section on Sal coming to friends and family, there are several rainbow stories. I have amazing rainbow stories as well. Sometimes just thinking of Sal as I look out the window, a rainbow might appear when I least expect it. I remember one time just recently, as I was looking out and thinking of Sal and how the most important thing to me in life is to love and be loved, and as I spoke those words to a friend on the phone, the sky outside the window lit up with a beautiful double rainbow, in an area that doesn't usually get rainbows and it was sunny and beautiful out. Sometimes Sal's rainbows come with a healing energy as in the case of Lauren and Dustin. Sometimes they come with messages of great wisdom. I only mention a few rainbow stories, as Lauren and Dustin write about rainbows in the friend section.

Rainbows of Wisdom

Don't Take Anything Personally. Nothing others do is because of you. What others say and do is a projection of their own reality, their own dream.

–DON MIGUEL RUIZ, AUTHOR—THE FOUR AGREEMENTS

It was just days before the Celebration of Life event for Sal was to take place and just about two weeks after Sal made his transition. My life at this point was completely filled with synchronicities; everything I needed was just showing up without much effort on my part. It had to be this way since I only had six days to put this entire celebration together.

During this time, something very destructive was said to me. I had to leave the house from this blow. I went into my yoga/meditation studio in the garden to attempt to catch my breath. As I sat on the floor of the studio, I notice the room was filling up with rainbows! There were little round rainbows everywhere in the room on all four walls. And they were moving clockwise around the walls of the room. I was caught off guard, by this brilliant display of vibrant light and color. The rainbows were accompanied by a feeling of comfort. But what was even more astonishing was the message that was coming from Sal loud and clear in my head. It was not a voice I could hear with my ears but a download I could *feel* with my *heart*.

Sal was saying, *it's ok, you do not need to take this in. This is not about you, it is about the other. Do not take this personally because it isn't personal, in fact it never is. What others do is a projection of their own beliefs and does not reflect you. When you learn not to take in the insults and opinions of others, you will not suffer and you will not be a victim. You will know better the next time it happens and it will go right through you.*

Sal told me that I was doing an amazing job on his celebration, and I could return to the positive high vibration I was in before this happened. I just needed to rest. I took a short nap amongst the swirling rainbows and woke up feeling healed from the trauma that I took in. The nap with the rainbows acted as a reset button to rid me of the negative feelings and bring me back to the feelings of love.

I learned throughout the following months and years to never take anything personal. Sal came to me again later to remind me of this truth. It was a lesson I needed to learn. I was a people-pleaser most of my life, always putting myself behind everyone else in order to keep harmony in the family. I felt I could handle anything, but I needed to protect and please everyone around me. I would be happy if I knew everyone else was happy. I did not realize the toll this was taking on me. I am now learning how important it is to have boundaries and honor and take care of myself .

Sal's Presence & Rainbow Waves

Out beyond ideas of wrongdoing and right doing there is a field.
I'll meet you there. When the soul lies down in that grass, the world
is too full to talk about.

–RUMI, THIRTEENTH-CENTURY SCHOLAR AND POET

Journal Notes: December 16, 2013

Sal's birthday is December 12th and my birthday is only four days later, on December 16th. The year Sal was born, 1988, I was given my best birthday present ever, a newborn baby. Sal was my first of two children, both of them boys. We took Sal home in a big felt Christmas stocking the volunteers at the hospital had handmade. The day Sal was born was the happiest day of my life. The other happiest day is when Arthur was born. I have always felt that babies are our greatest gift.

Sal always gave me the greatest birthday presents. Sal dreamt big and he was generous, giving gifts gave him such joy. I had always wanted a fireplace in my bedroom. One day in early November, just weeks before he passed. Sal came over and said his contractor friend was going to meet us at the house and give Sal an estimate on a fireplace. As it turned out the contractor was not able to make it. I told Sal that I felt that present was just too big. I told him all I wanted for my birthday was to spend the whole day with him, just being together and doing something fun. He just smiled, I'm not sure what he was thinking, but I think I probably would have gotten my day with Sal and a fireplace!

I was completely exhausted after organizing the Celebration of Life event for Sal, not to mention my entire being was still aching from being in shock. I had never given a thought to what I would do if a family member passed. However, the most sacred event just flowed its way to me. Sal was an event planner and I felt him joining me and guiding my every decision. I actually felt him be excited about this event. It was on his twenty-fifth birthday, and I knew our focus together was to turn traditional sad funeral services into rich celebrations of life. To let everyone there know there is no death, no annihilation, but a continuation of an expanded life. We made a professional movie of his life; his friend Kelsey, worked on this movie day and night to have it done in time. We also made twenty-five poster boards of his life in action. I was always a camera buff so we had tons of photos to choose from. I have friends who are talented musicians, a sound healer, a minister, and so forth. They all stepped up to create a beautiful and heart-felt event to honor the life of Sal.

So by the time my birthday came, only four days later, I was exhausted. My birthday fell on a Monday, and on Monday mornings, I go to my friend Gail's house for her yoga and meditation class. It happened to be the most exquisite morning I have ever seen on the Central Coast. To this day I have never experienced such a magnificent day on the coast. The way the sun was shining so bright in the early morning, the warm gentle breeze caressing my face, the bright blue sky, and the birds chirping, it was just glorious. And then I laughed to myself as *I remembered last night before I fell asleep, I asked Sal to give me a sunny day for my birthday,* as we get lots of fog on the Central California Coast.

I had gotten to class early and I saw Gail out on the back deck over the ocean, doing some energization exercises. Gail is an advanced soul and she looked beautiful with the ocean below her. Her house literally sits on the ocean and during the high tides the ocean goes under the house.

I laid down my mat in the house and did not disturb her. I decided to take a walk on the coastside trail, since I was early for class. It was such an unusually warm morning on the beach. I walked by the Miramar restaurant along the beach and I just couldn't believe the beauty of this day. I overheard two restaurant workers as they were doing some work outside in front of the restaurant. They were speaking in Spanish and saying "Are we in Mexico?" I chuckled to myself at their joke and kept walking.

As I began to walk slowly, taking in the beauty and feeling gratitude in my heart, I began to feel Sal's presence. It was as though he was right next to me with his arm around me, as we so often walked together this way. I sat down on a lone bench near where we use to have the Fourth of July parties on the beach. I got lost in meditation and the bliss of being in this world, but not of this world. I loved spending this time with just Sal and me. I was walking along the beach now back to Gail's but I could not leave this beautiful walk with Sal so I continued on. I left the trail and went down on to the sandy beach and sat on a log and stayed immersed in my time with Sal. And then he reminded me, *Remember you said you just wanted to spend the whole day with me? And here we are.* I know I could have been sad, but I was so uplifted and filled again with this unconditional love.

It was getting to be noon as I glanced at my phone, I had been here since 8 a.m. I knew for my birthday, my friends were probably waiting for me with a birthday cake. I went back to Gail's to join them; they had looks on their faces like, *Oh my god, what do I say to a mother who just lost her son.* They were surprised to find me in a blissful state. They did have cake, lunch, and presents for me. But their real gift was their love and caring nature.

And then Sal gave us all a present, another rainbow miracle. As we looked out from Gail's window, *each and every wave had its own individual little dancing rainbow* right above the wave! We were all in awe and none of us had ever seen anything like it before. Nor have I ever seen anything like it again. What could have been a very sad and heavy birthday, turned out to be a most joyous and uplifting event for everyone present. Not only did

Sal and I spend the day together as promised just a month before, but he also sent dancing rainbows above each wave for everyone present to enjoy. Thank you Sal!

Later that evening when the sun went down and we went out to dinner for my birthday with my family and Denise, my childhood best friend, I did feel sad and I really missed Sal. It was still so fresh and it was my first birthday without Sal. It was only three weeks since he passed. I allowed myself to feel the sadness fully and let it pass through me. Again acceptance was my only intelligent choice. I don't want to give the impression that it was all good, it wasn't, but the palpable presence of Sal and the dancing rainbow waves were truly a blessing that eased the pain of the giant hole in my heart.

Ask and It Is Given

I am realistic – I expect miracles.

–WAYNE W. DYER, AUTHOR

Journal Notes, November 15, 2015

Today I took Rosie for a beach walk, as I walked down the long staircase to the beach, a strange familiar feeling came over me. I realized this beautiful November day was exactly like the day I walked Rosie on this exact beach the day Sal passed, just nine days short of two years ago. It was the same kind of day, unusually warm for November and only one other person on the entire beach sitting on the rocks near the bottom of the steps. With the two-year anniversary coming up, my body jumped right into reliving the experience of going into shock, I was physically feeling the memory in my body again. It was not something I consciously did, it just happened physically. I know this happened last year around the same time. It is just something to observe and doesn't need to be labeled as good or bad.

There is nothing either good or bad but thinking makes it so.

–WILLIAM SHAKESPEARE

This was the same beach on which I saw the "message in the sand" I wrote about in Part I. As always I enjoy constant reassurance from Sal that he is here with me. I walked on the beach thinking of him and how grateful I am having sons like him and Arthur. I asked Sal to give some sign today to let me know he is here and to relieve the memory of the shock. I asked him to play with me, with, well, maybe rainbows.

It was a casual request and it was playful. I let the request go into the ethers of the universe and forgot about it. But as soon as I got in my car, there were little vibrating rainbows all over the inside of my car, on the dashboard, the steering wheel, the seats, and inside of the front doors. And yes, I have a crystal hanging from the mirror, but these little round rainbows were so vivid and they were all over. The sun has to be just at the right angle and it has to be just the right time of day for this to occur. I'm not sure I have ever seen rainbows from this crystal before. I just laughed and went on with my day. I went to get my car washed in the drive-through carwash, and as soon as I entered, a huge rainbow flashed in front of me! Ok, yes it sprays water and water and sun can make an instant rainbow. But the sun rays have to hit it just perfectly and it has to be a certain time of day. I have been through this carwash hundreds of times and have never seen a rainbow here. Ok, it's getting more and more playful and fun now.

Next I go into the local grocery store and I see rainbows all over in there. Is the light just right for rainbows everywhere I go? I continue to see little rainbows for the rest of the day. With all these validations and fun signs, the feeling of shock was gone and has never returned. Sal was always so much fun on earth, it is just who he naturally is, but the cool thing is that he is just as fun, if not more fun, from the formless realm!

Sal, love you to the sun and back, a trillion times!

Sal's Infinite Creativity

And we are put on this earth a little space,
that we may learn to bear the beams of love.

–William Blake, English Poet

This sign came just yesterday; I am almost done writing this book, but just had to add this sign because it is such a funny one and quite amazing.

I decided to take a break with my friend, Kelsey, and go on a hike in the nearby forest. On the Central California Coast, October is the nicest month. It was one of those rare warm balmy autumn days in the redwood forest. It almost feels like you are in a magical place, not on this planet. It feels like nowhere I've ever been. The air feels so good on your skin and it smells so good in the forest in this warm air. But just a few more steps can take you into another blissful atmosphere of cooler, refreshing air. It can change temperature like when you are swimming in a stream with hot springs underneath the ground, the water temperature changes from one location to the next.

On this particular day, it was extra magical in the forest. We came to the opening in the forest where Sal first contacted me, two days after his transition. I was pointing this out to Kelsey, when we noticed the maple trees in this area, shedding giant leafs of warm hues of autumn colors. They were slowly swirling to the ground in a perfect unison, as though putting on a show for us. We stood there in awe, one because it was a beautiful sight to behold, and two, it was going on for a long time. We were amazed and at the same time, we both reached for our cell phones to take a video of this beautiful dance of red, orange, and yellow blends of maple leaves. But by the time we found our phones in our backpacks, the wind had stopped. I wondered if this unusually beautiful show of free-form dancing leaves could be part of Sal's signs. There did not seem to be enough leaves on the trees for it to be raining leaves for so long and it was in the exact spot he first came to me. And he loves when I hang out with Kelsey. Sal and Kelsey met in middle school and became immediate friends. They remained close friends throughout his entire life.

We hiked up a narrow, winding trail and found a beautiful, tall bridge over a flowing creek. We found an area of comfortable, cushy foliage of dried pine needles and redwood sorrel and made that our resting spot. We decided to take ten minutes to sit in silence and take in the smells and sounds, as we breathed in the warm air of the forest. Some call this forest bathing. It is just slowing down and absorbing the comforts that nature offers. As I was sitting in silence with closed eyes, I felt Sal's presence; I joked with him and said, "Hey send us a rainbow!" I do not ask Sal for signs very often, especially now because I have become accustomed to feeling his presence and trusting my knowing. I thought it would be fun to get a rainbow since two people he loved were together, and Kelsey and I love to get rainbows from Sal. I knew it would be impossible as it was a dry and warm day. But practical things like that usually do not deter Sal.

I forgot about my request and did not think to mention to Kelsey that I had silently asked Sal to send us a rainbow. As we were driving home, we passed the fire station. Kelsey exclaimed, "Oh my god, look at that huge rainbow!" The firemen, for some reason had the fire hose and were shooting it straight up into the sky, creating the giant rainbow. I have lived here for twenty-eight years and drive by the firehouse all the time and have never seen this before. I told her I had asked Sal to send us one. I slowed down the car as we both gazed up at the giant rainbow high up in the sky and burst into laughter, knowing that I had asked Sal for a rainbow on a hot, dry day! I never knew that Sal would keep me laughing even when he was not in body. I will never get tired of these signs. It is how he rolls now in the formless realm.

Coastside Path

Synchronicity takes the coincidence of events in space and time as meaning something more than mere chance.

–CARL JUNG, SWISS PSYCHIATRIST

While I was spending some focused time writing this book, I asked Sal to give me a sign, just for fun. Later that day I took a break from writing and went for a walk on the coastside trail. Many people were out exercising on the trail, biking, walking, and running. A man ran right by me with a black t-shirt with big, bold white letters that read, Heart of a Lion. This was unbelievable for two reasons: first because that is the same exact name of my one of favorite songs that Sal wrote and those exact words are in the chorus. And second, Sal knows for me to see it, it had to be in big letters with white and black, because I have an eye condition, where I do not see well if there is not sufficient contrast. And of course, black and white is the best for contrast. Sal knew he had a heart of a lion and I know that is why he wrote that song.

As if the one sign wasn't fun enough already and a LOL sign from Sal, he managed to send me another awesome sign. As I walked further down the path, there was a rainbow on the ground; it was a patch of a rainbow, out of nowhere. So I knew Sal was playing with me or maybe it was just a random rainbow that I could not figure out where it was coming from. Anyway, I decided to take a photo of it for my rainbow collection. When I got home and looked at the photo on my phone, the image of my head was completely black and placed right in the middle of the vivid rainbow path, making for a very interesting and beautiful photo.. What I think happened is that when I took the photo of the rainbow patch, my shadow got in the photo and my head somehow landed right on the rainbow patch. Humm….interesting and very cool, I thought. Maybe Sal …? He has a way of doing amazing things with light!

I now know when it is Sal because I have learned to feel him, and to be more confident in my knowing. Yes, it was Sal!

The Reflection

For the outer sense alone perceives visible things and the eye of the heart alone sees the invisible.

–RICHARD OF SAINT VICTOR, MEDIEVAL SCOTTISH PHILOSOPHER

Every year on Sal's birthday, it is a time to celebrate him and remember how special he made all of us feel in his presence. It was December 12,

2015, and we had a meditation for Sal at the Sanctuary of Peace that is dedicated to him on Ananda Valley Farm in Half Moon Bay. It was a beautiful tribute to him and now we were back at our home in Half Moon Bay having a casual potluck dinner. I was standing near the kitchen table with a plate full of food in my hands and talking to a friend. Behind my friend, on the wall hangs a large glass-framed picture.

As I'm talking to my friend, I am noticing that there is a reflection of a happy face in the glass. As I look a little closer while still giving this person my attention, as to not be rude, I see it is Sal! He is laughing and smiling at me. I see it clearly for about twenty seconds. I am so blown away that I don't even speak, but just listen to this person. I laugh to myself and thank Sal for making an appearance. I don't even mention it to the person I am speaking with because it is a gift from Sal to me and because this surreal life is now becoming more and more normal for me. It brings a slight smile to my lips and a sparkle to my eyes, which remains for the rest of the day. That enlightened smile of knowing, all is well and a knowing that nothing is really as it appears to be.

We Fly With Sal!

*The intuitive mind is a sacred gift and the rational mind
is a faithful servant. We have created a society that honors the servant
and has forgotten the gift.*

–ALBERT EINSTEIN

Eight months after Sal's transition, our family decided to take a vacation to Costa Rica. I was grateful to have this time for our family to bond, relax and have some time together to talk about Sal as much as we wanted to. We were in gratitude to be able to take this adventurous vacation together, and I was especially thankful to take Arthur, as he had always wanted to explore Costa Rica because of the wildlife, the rainforest, and the diversity of this gorgeous country. On June 28, 2014, we headed to Costa Rica, we were flying for the first time on Sun Country airline. And a totally unexpected sign appeared as we entered the airplane. On the floor in front of me I saw a white light in the shape of a sitting meditator; this was quite astonishing and was a beautiful image to behold. I have been teaching meditation since Sal was a small child; I knew this particular sign was for our family and was from Sal, and I caught it right away. Sal was getting more creative as he plays with light and makes magic happen, it wasn't just rainbows anymore.

Then I looked at the wall right above the meditator of white light and I saw a poster with a picture of a lion that said, "Today you're flying with Sal!" It was printed exactly as I printed it here with the exclamation mark and all. That totally blew all of us away. Again Sal, with this poster and those words from Sal the lion, was giving us validation that the meditator of light was a sign from him, and obviously the poster was a big sign as well.

I thought about the mountain lion and there was even more significance. One of my favorite songs written by Sal had a chorus that goes like this: "Heart of a *lion*, feel like I'm *flying*!" On top of that, less than a year before Sal passed, we had two baby mountain lion cubs take refuge in our garden. This incident made national news and is a story for another time. But between the mountain lion, the written message of flying with Sal, and the meditator of light, there was no doubt that Sal was using all kinds of signs to reach his family.

After everyone was seated, I went back and took photos of both the meditator made of light and the poster saying, "Today you're flying with Sal!"

Wow, again this was a LOL display of creativity that Sal was with his family on this Costa Rican family vacation. Sal made sure from the beginning of this first family vacation without him, to send us signs with his usual validation that he was absolutely with his family but formless. Further, on this particular trip, Sal came to me in the early mornings, daily, through the Costa Rican giant morphic blue butterfly as you will see in the butterfly section.

Hearts of Light

Your vision will become clear only when you can look into your own heart.
Who looks outside, dreams; who looks inside, awakes.

–CARL JUNG, SWISS PSYCHIATRIST, AUTHOR

Shortly after Sal made his transition, we all started seeing rainbows every-where. But after a while it wasn't just rainbows, it was also hearts of white light. Sometimes these would appear in a dark room with no outside light. It usually happened in my bedroom just before bedtime, but not always.

One time when I walked in my home after being away for several weeks, I saw the most astonishing thing. As you walk in the back door, and look straight ahead I have a large framed photo of Sal swimming with a dolphin. Sal is underwatee diving downward, with a dolphin leading the way. A beautiful heart of white light appeared on the photo where his own physical heart would be!

I did have a heart hanging in the kitchen that could have reflected this. But what are the chances that I would walk in right at the exact time that this could appear. I looked for it again at the same time the next few evenings and it was not there. I have never seen this happen again. From my experience with Sal, it appears spirits know how to use light to delight us and let us know they are near.

Hearts Everywhere!

About four months or less after Sal passed I started seeing hearts every-where. I would be taking a walk and see beautiful leafs on the sidewalk in my neighborhood that were in the shape of a perfect heart. Or I would see seashells on the beach that were heart-shaped. I would see rocks on my hikes in the woods that were in the shape of perfectly shaped hearts. I also saw cloud formations that were in the shape of hearts. Even when I would squeeze my body lotion out in the palm of my hand it would form a perfect heart! And most amazing was the hearts of white light that would appear on walls in my home, even if the room was dark. It seemed the universe was showing me hearts everywhere I looked!

As I have mentioned Sal has kept his sense of humor. During this phase of seeing hearts everywhere. I notice that our pet dog, Rosie, was pooping in the shape of hearts. But then. Lauren who now had Sal's dog was also pooping in the shape of a heart. We started texting photos back and forth of doggie poop hearts! It was a little crazy, but this is what happened.

As my own heart cracked open and was expanding I was seeing hearts everywhere in my physical reality. I felt it was Sal and the universe showing me I was loved and that love and compassion are the way, the only way to be in this universe, whether you are form or formless. It was fun and playful, and I still see hearts now in many unexpected places.

CHAPTER FIVE:

Blue Butterflies, Hugs, and Numbers

Blue Butterflies Abound!

What the caterpillar calls the end of the world, the master calls the butterfly.

–RICHARD BACH, AUTHOR

About eight months after Sal made his transition, our family decided to take a trip to Costa Rica. We just wanted to have some down time and bond as a family. It did turn out to be a wonderful trip, we carried Sal with us in our hearts.

Whenever I am home or away, my favorite part of the day is the early mornings. I like to have some quiet time to myself while most of the world is still asleep This was especially fun to do in Costa Rica because of the beauty and diversity of nature that country holds.

On the trip I would get up before my husband and my son. I would enjoy my early morning meditation in the alluring nature of Costa Rica. Sometimes I would be sitting on a beach, hiking in a forest, relaxing in a warm pool, or sipping tea on a mountaintop. But no matter where I was for my morning meditation in Costa Rica, a large, enchanting blue butterfly would be fluttering around me and in the vicinity I was in. The common name for these butterflies is the blue morpho.

These blue butterflies look illusory; their wings are a vibrant iridescent blue, and the wingspan can be up to eight inches. You only see the bright iridescent blue when they flutter their wings. As the morning sun would reflect off their wings, a flash of bright metallic blue would be revealed. It looked as though their wings were lit up. It was always impossible to photograph this with my camera because of their quick and somewhat erratic movements. When they landed they close their wings. When they fold their wings together, you could see only the outside, which was a brown color with some darker brown spots. They blended in perfectly with the leaves and branches where they landed. It becomes evident that Mother Nature made the outside of their wings to be camouflage with the elements for their protection. You only saw the electric iridescent blue as they fluttered around, like mystical fairies in the forest.

Every time I would see them I would feel Sal's energy very strongly. I loved this experience. It felt so good and so reassuring that he is showing me signs and that he is still here with us.

No matter what part of the island we were on, I would see one every morning. It wasn't until later that I learned they are quite rare to see. And every time they came to be in stillness with me, I felt the soul essence of my beloved Sal.

The funny thing is when I got back home, I kept seeing blue butterflies everywhere, not necessarily real Costa Rican giant blue morphos flying around. But they appeared on websites I was looking at and cards people would give me. I went to the mall and giant paper blue butterflies were above me hanging from the ceiling. I began to notice them around my house, on brochures that came in the mail, on stamps and stickers, on teapots, walls in restaurants, even on the wallpaper in a public bathroom! These blue butterflies seemed to be everywhere.

A few months after our trip, Arthur and I decided to take a day off and to check out the Academy of Science in San Francisco. The theme of the museum was the blue morpho! They were flying around everywhere in the rainforest section and were flying all around me, one even landed on me! It was so much fun. And the round sticker they gave us for becoming members that day was of, you guessed it, a blue butterfly.

Finally, I Remember!

Synchronicity appears when a symbol that has been personally meaningful suddenly proves - or acts in accord with - it's significance.

–DAVID RICHO, PHD, AUTHOR

I would feel Sal's presence very strongly, every time I saw a blue butterfly. I wasn't sure why I was feeling him associated with blue butterflies. And why since he passed was I seeing them everywhere? And then it hit me, when I least expected it. I was messaging, Dave, a good friend of Sal's who regularly posts rainbows from Sal on Facebook. Dave sees these as he travels the world. He feels Sal as he sees these rainbows, as do many others. I was telling him how I see blue butterflies and feel Sal. As I was telling him, the reason why I feel Sal when I see blue butterflies, came to me like a lightning bolt!

Awhile back on Mother's Day, I had a wonderful day with Sal and Arthur. Sal was twenty-one and Arthur was eighteen. We were at Sal's apartment in San Francisco. Sal was attending USF at the time. Sal and Arthur were making me a delicious gourmet Mother's Day brunch, of lobster cooked in beer. Some fancy recipe Sal had found on the internet. Wow, I thought what a lucky mom, both my boys slaving away in the kitchen, while I sipped on a mimosa, relaxing on the couch. Then Sal announced that we were going to go shopping for my Mother's Day present on Haight Street. He said it was where all the cool stuff was that I would like. In the past for my birthday, he had bought me a very cool wall hanging for my yoga studio. And another time for Christmas a huge wooden dragon head carving from Tibet. Both of these wonderful gifts were purchased by Sal at the Haight-Ashbury district. So I thought that sounded like a great idea. I was down to hit the old hippie section of the city.

The three of us headed to the Haight-Ashbury neighborhood in Sal's old beat-up Mazda. As we were cruising, slowing to look for a parking place, the two of them see Mama's Tattoo's, they are now both ecstatic. They are telling me the shop even has the perfect name for a mother's day present. They are saying we could all three get a tattoo to bond us for life! I'm thinking wait! What happen to sipping mimosas on the couch? I wasn't planning on being tortured on Mother's Day! And I never had a desire to get a tattoo at all.

They were so enthusiastic about this tattoo idea and going on and on about how fun and cool this was going to be. I hadn't seen them this excited since I bought them Pokémon cards and beanie babies! The thought of being bonded for life through a tattoo touched my heart though. Wow, in retrospect, am I glad now I went through with it.

They were talking about all three of us getting the Sicilian flag. I am full-blooded Sicilian, and they are half. I love being Sicilian; however, I did not want the flag on my body! I told them the only thing I would tattoo on my body was a butterfly.

Butterflies have always represented transformation to me. I have read several of Elisabeth Kübler-Ross's books. And I remember being so touched when she spoke of the graffiti on the walls of the holding rooms in concentration camps. These are the rooms the Jewish prisoners were held in before they were made to enter the gas chambers.

There were random simple sketches of butterflies in all the holding chambers. It did not matter which country the camp was in. It was in all of the camps she visited. It was as though the souls of these prisoners had a knowing of the freedom and transition they were about to experience.

Butterflies also represent transformation from creepy crawlers to graceful, radiant, winged creatures. To me they represented the transformation of our physical selves into nonphysical infinite spirits. Because of my interpretation of the butterfly, it makes perfect sense that Sal would choose butterflies as a symbol to reach me. But it is more than that.

So…. the three of us decided that I would get a tattoo on my ankle of three butterflies, one mama with two babies, which would represent the three of us. Sal held my hand through the whole process as we laughed and joked around. When it came time to pick the colors for our butterflies, I picked my favorite color, purple. Arthur was down the hall getting his own tattoo. While still holding my hand, Sal was yelling down the hall to ask

Arthur what color he wanted, Arthur shouted back, green. (Our presence livened up the whole place!) And, you guessed it, Sal picked his butterfly to be the color, BLUE. Sal had sparkling blue eyes so he probably figured blue would be a good color to represent him.

I *realized*, here I had been walking around with a *blue butterfly* tattooed on my ankle that *represented Sal*. It's no wonder I feel Sal when I see blue butterflies! I feel our loved ones are always playing little games with us to let us know they are near. I would also like to add here that even if I did not have a blue butterfly on my body representing Sal, it would still be Sal I was feeling when I saw these butterflies. We need to trust our intuitive feelings. But because I really like the validation, the universe seems to constantly give it to me.

My friend, Gail, works almost daily on the Ananda Valley Farm. This is an organic vegetable farm run by volunteers. With the help of many hands, we built a sanctuary dedicated to Sal on this sacred land, hidden in a gorgeous valley, just a few miles inland from the sea. I was talking to Gail on the phone while she was working at the farm. We were talking about Sal when suddenly, she said, "Oh my God, I am getting swarmed here by blue butterflies!" This has happened on more than one occasion! And it is usually when we are planning an event around Sal at the yurt, which I have named the "The Sanctuary of Peace."

I constantly see blue butterflies to this day. Just last night I was sipping some delicious tea in a dainty teacup, which was a gift from a dear friend, given to me shortly after Sal passed. As I was enjoying drinking out of this beautiful teacup, I notice it had an adorable ladybug, a bumblebee, flowers, and a butterfly on it. And yes, the butterfly was blue! It has been uncanny how these blue butterflies are constantly showing up in my life.

I just have to smile, when these things happen. Through my connection with Sal, I now have a direct line to, what the author, Pam Grout calls the FP. The FP stands for infinite Field of Possibilities, also known as God. Knowing that as we tap into the nonphysical, the veil between the formless realm and us physical humans becomes thin. And the potential for life to become a lot more fun and lighthearted emerges. Another thing that just happens without any effort is that you lose your fear of death. You begin to realize there is no ending to us, no death, and no separation.

An Unusual Butterfly!

*We delight in the beauty of the **butterfly**, but rarely admit the changes it has gone through to achieve that beauty."*

–MAYA ANGELOU, AUTHOR, ACTRESS

From early spring until the end of fall, I start most days with a morning hike in the redwood forest near my house. I prefer the forest to a gym, and for me the benefits of the forest are unmatched by any other environment. Numerous studies have shown that exercising at and even just being in the forest energizes us, promotes mental clarity and a sense of well-being. This is partly due to the increase in the number of negative ions in the forest, especially if there is a stream. For me nature is the best place to feel my connection with Source and it is also the place I feel Sal very strongly.

At the end of the trail near the parking lot, there are restrooms that I usually need to use after my hike. One morning as I was using the facilities, I looked on the ground and there, right in front of me, was the most beautiful butterfly made out of toilet paper on the cement floor! I laughed out loud! This was a perfectly made butterfly out of a random piecec of toilet paper that had fallen to the ground in the rustic restroom; all for my enjoyment! The scraps of toilet paper were somehow formed into a butterfly.

Playful Butterflies

Awaken to the universes simple gift of the butterfly. Watch with fascination and joy as a jeweled treasure glides by and gently touches your soul.

–K. D'ANGELO, SINGER

This morning as I was getting up and checking emails on my computer, a photo of Sal popped up, it seemed to come out of nowhere. It was a photo I had never seen before. It was an adorable photo of him with his love, Lauren. They were dancing at Lauren's senior ball. I remember the evening well, taking photos of them all dressed up and looking great. Sal who loved to wear hats, had a cool white hat on that went great with his white linen suit. Sal's infectious smile made me feel his charismatic energy, and I could feel Lauren's contentment shining through her expressive deep brown eyes. Suddenly a flood of memories filled me from the past, and my heart broke as I burst into tears from the intense pain of missing Sal. My heart went out to Lauren.

After doing some meditation and a few stretches, I knew I had to head to the forest for a walk in solitude. It would have to be a quick walk as I had so much work to do today and was scheduled to teach soon. As I walked on the dirt path winding through the forest, Sal came to me, he told me that he is not in the past, he is available to me only in the present. He reminded me that life is only in the present and that the present was the only safe place to live. That in actuality there are no problems if we stay grounded in the present. And even if Sal were on earth today, that picture would still be a good time in the past. And once again I felt gratitude for all the incredibly beautiful memories I had shared with this beautiful soul in my life as an incredible son on earth and now as an incredible companion in the formless realm

As I continued to enjoy my walk, a beautiful, small blue butterfly started fluttering around me and I felt it was playing with me. I knew that this small blue butterfly was a sign from Sal, as his signature appearance to me is blue butterflies. When I was almost done with the walk, I playfully asked Sal to give me one more blue butterfly before I got into my car. I knew I was pushing the gift of getting signs and that at this point, I should be happy that I was feeling his communication and getting to see a blue butterfly, but it was quite playful. As I opened the trunk to get my purse out, I inwardly told Sal it doesn't have to be an actual butterfly, but a symbol or any creative way in which he could give me one more sign of a blue butterfly would add to the fun. As I closed the trunk, my eyes were drawn to a blue butterfly sticker on the bumper of the car next to mine! Ha ha, I could almost hear Sal laughing from the astral world and I laughed out loud here on earth. Again I was assured that playing with the spirit is so real and so possible when we place our awareness there.

Numbers Talk

We do not create our destiny; we participate in its unfolding. Synchronicity
works as a catalyst toward the working out of that destiny.

–DAVID RICHO, AUTHOR

The universe has lots of fun playing with us through numbers. In today's modern world, there are numbers everywhere we look, so it makes sense that numbers would be a good tool our past loved ones might use to reach us and play with us. Another modality to let us know they are still here with us. The number game started with me even before Sal passed. Numbers are also a way the universe can play with us. The power of coincidence and synchronicity are a way in which life shows us what we need to know.

Numbers become a language of their own and it is *our* interpretation of what these numbers mean to us. Before Sal passed, the universe was playing with me through numbers. I started noticing that the number 333 was popping up everywhere for me. I would wake up in the middle of the night and it would be 3:33 am or I would check my phone for the time and it would be 3:33 pm. I would see the 3's on taxis, on license plates of cars in front of me. My friend Karen asked me while visiting her in Florida, what number the SPF was on my sunscreen, I looked and it was 33! Her response was, "Of course it is!"

I decided to look this phenomenon up on the internet to see what it might mean, although I knew it meant that I was in the flow, and in alignment with the universe. But I wanted some validation to confirm my intuitive thoughts on numbers and the way the universe was playing with me. I was shocked and delighted at what came up. Although lots of references come up when you search, I always pick one that I am guided to and I know that is the right one for me. I was led to a website by Doreen Virtue, an author and speaker. She wrote that 3's mean the ascended masters are here for you, like Jesus, Mary, and Yogananda! The fact that she named Yogananda was surprising to me, because I first became aware of Paramahansa Yogananda long ago during my yoga and meditation teacher training at the Expanding Light Retreat Center in Northern California. I resonated with Yogananda immediately, and he has been a guiding light, teacher, and force in my life ever since. Sal's Sanctuary of Peace is at the lush sacred valley where Ananda has an organic vegetable farm. Ananda is an amazing group of devotees who follow the teachings of Paramahansa Yogananda and the four other Self-Realized, masters in that linage, including Jesus.

I was raised Catholic; therefore I was born into the teachings of Jesus. I had not resonated with the guilt and strict manmade rules of the religion. But I have a very strong resonance with Jesus, even as a very young child. Jesus was my first teacher and I have always felt his presence and his guidance in my life. And I have also always felt very connected to our divine Mother Mary, now more than ever as we both lost our sons. I love how she is in every neighborhood in Italy in hidden little alcoves.

This number thing became a fun game between me and the universe and the ascended masters, and then … I started seeing 444. Again 4's were everywhere, while I was still getting 3's.

So I went back to the internet and to Doreen Virtue's website on numbers. This time I found that 4's meant the angels are with me, guiding me. I loved this because my mother and I both loved angels. One of the best things the Catholic Church teaches children is that you have a guardian angel who is with you at all times. It teaches young children to tap in with the formless realm to feel safe, protected, and loved by their very own angel. I do not claim to know what angels really are. But I do know from direct experience that when I tap into the universal energy of angels, I usually receive the guidance I am asking for.

Sal often reaches me through numbers. One year had passed since Sal's transition and it was getting close to his twenty-sixth birthday. I was planning a celebration for him.

As I started thinking about Sal's birthday coming up, I started seeing 1212 everywhere! December 12th is Sal's birthday. Almost every day as I started planning the celebration for Sal whenever I looked at my phone it just happened to be 12:12. As it got near his birthday, I decided to put a photo of him on my cell phone as a screen saver. I chose a photo of him doing one of his favorite activities. Chilling out after a day of wakeboarding. The photo was a close up of his face, he looks relaxed and very content with life.

The thirty-foot yurt that was to be a sacred space for peace and dedicated to Sal was almost done. The synchronicities which came together to create this sacred space were many. A local contractor had heard about Sal's death and stepped up to manage this project, he had the professional equipment and know-how to build the platform on the side of a hill. It was completely built by a crew of volunteers.

It was not my idea to do this for Sal; it seemed to manifest seamlessly from start to finish. And now Sal gets to hang out with all the Masters.

A small group of us were going to enjoy our first meditation in the yurt. It wasn't quite finished, but it was up. Right as we were about to begin, one of the people in the group phone ran. He promptly turned of his phone, I thought, oh what a good reminder to turn off my own phone. When I pulled out my phone to turn it off, Sal's relaxed, smiling photo with the numbers 12:12 across it, popped up! If my friends phone did not randomly ring at exactly 12:12, this would have never happened. How is it that out of the one thousand four hundred and forty minutes in a day, it was exactly12:12 when we were christening Sal's Sanctuary of Peace with our first meditation in there? Again it is just his way of showing me, *I am here with you, life is good, relax. And this yurt thing is really cool, thanks.*

It's important to realize all the pieces that had to be put together to make this synchronicity happen for that one moment. We need to realize and appreciate the effort that goes into these signs from our loved ones and the universe, and to recognize the significance of these beautiful heartfelt signs. Realize this life is all about love, stay in gratitude, and watch the abundance of life's synchronicity all around you!

There are so many other signs having to do with numbers, but I will include just one more. I am with Arthur in his car and he asks me the time, so I look on my phone and laugh. I tell Arthur it's 12:12, Sal is here! Then we look at the time in his car on the dashboard and not only is it 12:12, it is also 12:12 88! It is early April in Hayward, a city by the San Francisco Bay that has very mild weather. It is very unusual for the temperature outside to be 88 degrees in early April. Sal was born on December 12, 1988. The time and outside temperature are right next to each other on the dashboard. So it shows as a display of not only the month and day he was born, but also the year he was born! Again this took some planning and maybe some manipulation to get this synchronicity to show up! It is with great delight, creativity, perfect timing, and humor that Sal delivers these signs.

I Get My REAL Sal Hug!

There is only one path to Heaven. On Earth, we call it Love.

–HENRY DAVID THOREAU, 1817, AMERICAN AUTHOR, PHILOSOPHER

November 12, 2014

Last night I finally had a very vivid and lucid dream of Sal, it was a wonderful dream! And the most fascinating part of the dream was that I was aware and awake in the dream. Before I fell asleep last night I told Sal that although I am doing well, I am really missing his physicality. He and Arthur both have the best hugs. And while I am so grateful to have Arthur in my life, I still really miss Sal and his wonderful warm bear hugs. I continued to tell Sal that in all honesty this vibrational relationship takes work and is not always easy, yet I must say, it is full of wonderful surprises that continue to amaze me. Yet, I just really, really miss your physicality and your hugs!

I fell off to sleep shortly after that discussion with Sal. And then I had the incredible dream that gave me such strong validation of Sal's presence in my life. In the dream I saw Sal—he looked happy, healthy and vibrant. He told me he was doing well and he gave me one of his Sal hugs. And I kept hugging him, saying, "You are real!" And he was laughing and saying, "Yes I am real!" Then we were both laughing and saying it over and over again.

I was conscious and I could feel him just as if he was standing here, right now. It was joyful, loving and so appreciated. This is what is called a lucid dream—when you are awake and aware in your dream. Many of Sal's friends have told me that they also have had lucid dreams of Sal. I have had several dreams of Sal; not all of them are lucid. When dreams are choppy and random, I feel that is just the subconscious mind working things out. But when dreams are lucid or so vivid that you remember them clearly, these are the dreams when our loved ones visit us. The yogis believe that every night we are awake in the formless realm when we go into deep sleep and our brains are in the slowest wave, called delta. They believe that this is when we visit with past loved ones, but most of the time we do not remember when we are in the deep sleep stages, which are different than dream states.

What I got from this hugging dream is that Sal is just as real as he ever was, just now in a formless state. "Sal I feel your awesome fun and loving spirit! You are the best! (Something he often said to me) I see you, I feel you! Thank you for coming to me and thank you for being my direct guide to who I truly am, Infinite Spirit!" We are all Infinite Spirit/ Infinite Intelligence. It is only in deep stillness that we realize who we truly are at our essence. Sal is my bridge of light to Source.

Breathe, Be Still and Know that I Am God.

–PSALM 46:10

CHAPTER SIX:

Special Occasions and Everyday Occurrences

No, I never saw an angel, but it is irrelevant whether I saw one or not.
I feel their presence around me.

–PAULO COELHO, AUTHOR

Sal Sends Love on Birthdays

Journal Notes: December 12, 2015, Sal's Birthday

We held a beautiful meditation and gathering today at Sal's Sanctuary of Peace to honor Sal on his birthday. Afterwards we had a potluck dinner at the house. It was quite an amazing day; Sal really came through with signs today. As we left the house to go to the yurt, we saw a vivid rainbow right in front of our house. We actually never see rainbows near our house. It was just a normal day, no rain or anything else that might precipitate a rainbow. We thought wow, what a great sign to start off this day.

But then we get to the yurt and there are some old helium balloons floating just above the entrance to the yurt. They had strings hanging from them but were not attached to anything. Happy Birthday was printed on them and they had blue butterflies on them! Many of us saw them but nobody had any idea where they came from. Another sign and the day had hardly begun!

Evan and Ashley, good friends of Sal's, attended the celebration at the yurt where many of Sal's family and friends shared their experiences of seeing rainbows from Sal, Evan is one of Sal's best friends all the way back to middle school. Ashley, Evan's girlfriend, was also very close with Sal. They had not received any signs from Sal. As they were driving down the old country road, leaving the yurt and heading to the house, Evan and Ashley saw their very own beautiful rainbow! It was just for them, they had left a little bit later than everyone else. It was wonderful to hear the enthusiasm in their voices as they told us of this vivid rainbow which they felt was a gift from Sal.

Sal's Surprise Appearance on Mother's Day!

Don't grieve. Anything you lose comes round in another form.

–RUMI, THIRTEENTH-CENTURY SCHOLAR AND POET

May 13, 2018

I spent Mother's Day with Arthur in his new home on the Oregon coast. The Oregon coast is absolutely gorgeous in May; the weather is warming up and the flowers are in full bloom. I woke up early like I do on most mornings and began my morning meditation.

Today was Mother's Day so it was especially important for me to feel Sal and my own mother. I felt him strong that morning in my meditation and it felt so good; it was all positive. I did not ask him for a sign but I did ask him to give something I had named, "Sal and Arthur energy." When the boys were young children, they would both want to sit next to me. When the three of us would snuggle on the bed to watch a movie, Sal would be on one side of me and Arthur on the other side. I would say, "I love this 'Sal/ Arthur energy!'" Or when we would walk holding hands I would say it again. So basically the term I coined, "Sal and Arthur energy," meant to us that Sal was on one side of me and Arthur was on the other side. It was a big loving energy on either side of me, and I felt lucky.

So that morning on Mother's Day, I simply asked, "Sal, give me some of that amazing 'Sal and Arthur energy'."

Arthur and I had a great morning, he took me out to a very cool place for breakfast called the Green Salmon. I had the best hot chocolate I have ever had; it was made with lavender and Mexican chocolate. It was a glorious sunny morning and the day was ours to explore this new area and have fun. We ended up in a nursery near his home that had blooming plants with large, vibrant purple and blue flowers. An unusually kind and knowledgeable saleswoman was helping us pick out some plants for Arthur's garden.

There was a beautiful tree with huge purple blossoms on it. The woman asked us if we would like her to take a photo of us standing under it. I thought that was a lovely idea and gave her my cell phone. Arthur put his arm around me for the photo and she snapped the shot. She handed me the phone, and I put it back in my purse. She helped us bring the plants up to the counter to purchase, but then left saying she actually was not an employee. She just loved plants and liked to help people pick out the perfect plants for their home garden. I thought, wow, this is a special woman, we were blessed to have her help.

We proceeded to have a wonderful day, going to the aquarium in Newport and walking in a beautiful forest that led right to the beach! Arthur planned many fun things for us to do. We were relaxing and having some delicious seafood for dinner when Arthur said, "Let's look at all the photos you took." As we were looking at my phone and laughing at all our funny photos of Buddy (Arthur's dog) and silly photos from the aquarium, we got to the first photo of the day at the nursery under the flowering tree of giant purple blossoms. The colors in this photo were more vivid than normal and looked surreal. This was taken with an iPhone with no enhancements. But the most surprising feature of this photo was a laser beam of bright white light coming out of my hand, and going into the earth. My hand was curled around this beam of light, it was holding on to the beam of white light. I immediately asked Arthur what is that thing coming out of my hand. And without any hesitation he said, *It's a beam of light.*

Sure enough it was showing me the "Sal and Arthur energy!" The gift I had asked Sal for on this Mother's Day. I had already been feeling it all day but as usual Sal gave me a huge, unbelievable sign to validate my intuitive knowing. It was a brilliant focused beam of light. It is on the cover of this book, still without any enhancements. I wanted the photo to be the original shot.

This was one of the most spectacular signs Sal has sent me. My thoughts went back to the angelic woman who seemed to come out of nowhere and was so informative about all the plants and then took this photo of us. Then she disappeared as fast as she had appeared.

Once again Sal gave me a priceless Mother's Day present from beyond, as he plays with light. But this gift was not only for me, it was for his brother, Arthur, and to all of you reading this book.

A Mysterious Buzz

There are only two ways to live your life. One is as though nothing is a miracle. The other is as though everything is a miracle."

–ALBERT EINSTEIN

Journal Notes: December 13, 2018

Like each year since Sal's passing, this year we will continue our tradition of celebrating Sal on his birthday. I woke up this morning feeling sad and missing Sal. Today was Sal's thirtieth birthday; he was so advanced at twenty-four, humm … what would he be doing today on his thirtieth birthday. Right away I caught myself and had to stop that kind of fruitless thinking. I have to remember to stay present and know that Sal is ageless and is still real and with me now, just in a different way. Thoughts like that lead to regret, grief, and pain.

I taught an early morning class and as always, it felt good to teach yoga. My yoga classes are more about presence than anything else, and as I hold an intense state of presence for my students, it keeps me anchored in the now—truly the only place where life exits and where problems dissolve. As I held this for the class, the wonderful effects of "Being" naturally began to show up. These affects are a calmness that sweeps over you and an enjoyment of life that comes from within and is independent of outside situations.

We had a really nice evening gathering in Sal's honor. His birthday being a week before Christmas is always a busy time for people to attend these celebrations. But I'm grateful that family and friends show up and tell me how important this gathering is for all of them too. I am deeply touched to see how many people love Sal so much and how cool it is that he is still bringing us all together. After dinner we all sat in a circle in the living room. We told stories about Sal while on earth and after earth. How he had reached us from beyond the physical, from the nonphysical.

His presence was palpable. Anyway, after everyone left it was about 11:45 pm, by midnight, I was in bed. I was almost asleep when I heard a buzzing sound from downstairs; it was a sound I have never heard before. It wasn't too loud and through wishful rational, I thought maybe I would be able to just sleep through it. But, I knew I had to check out what was going on, so I dragged myself out of bed and headed downstairs. It was dark downstairs except for the electric candle that burns twenty-four/seven on the little golden shelf right below Sal's portrait at the bottom of the stairs. I saw those beautiful bright blue eyes smiling at me, as his face was glowing from the soft glow of the candle.

The buzzing got louder as I approached the bottom of stairs; it seemed to be coming out of Sal's portrait! But then I realized it was the electric heater that buzzes when it is on uneven terrain. But how did it get right below Sal's portrait? After everyone left, before going to bed, I had checked it and it was in the living room and it was off! I left it plugged in and it was still plugged in the same outlet. But how did it get turned on and how did it get under Sal's portrait??

These unexplainable strange occurrences are now commonplace in my life, since Sal has been my constant companion. I laughed and asked Sal how he does this stuff. But the real clincher is after turning it off, I went back upstairs and got into bed; I asked Alexa what time it was, she answered, 12:13. Which means the buzzing was going off at precisely 12:12! Sal's birthdate, on the night of his thirtieth birthday. Of course the 12:12

was the usual added validation aspect of his sign. Just like when he was on earth, he never misses a beat! I had to write this in my journal the very next morning, while it was fresh in my mind.

A Mystifying Tune

When one sees eternity in the things that pass away,
and infinity in finite things, one has pure knowledge.

–BHAGAVAD GITA, SANSKRIT SCRIPTURE

We had our sixth annual gathering to honor Sal on Sal's thirty-first birthday. We had a houseful of guests as usual. Arthur and I cooked all day, making delicious food to honor Sal and nourish our family, neighbors, and friends. It was so nice to have Arthur home this year and help prepare the food; we laughed and joked around as we worked hard cooking.

Once again our love for Sal brought us all together. It is Sal's strong spirit that pulls all of us together and I know for sure he is feeling the love. Our formless loved ones know when we are celebrating them, and I know with Sal, he loves it and appreciates it.

After we had dinner, we all sat in a circle in the living room and we shared all the fun signs Sal has been sending us through the years. I talked about many of the topics in this book, which led to good conversation and helpful insights. It was so nice to see everyone and share this special day together.

My sister, Sally, and her family had spent the night in a nearby bed and breakfast in town. The following morning, I was rushing off to walk downtown to meet them for breakfast. It was early and Arthur was still sleeping. As I sat at the bottom of the stairs to put my shoes on, I heard a tune, it was a tune I had never heard before. At the bottom of the steps is Sal's portrait. If you remember from his last birthday, the buzzing from the portable radiant heater was going off spontaneously, right below his portrait. This year music was playing, which seemed to be coming out of his portrait. I figured Arthur must have left his cell phone somewhere near there and it was a ringtone from his phone. I looked all around but could not find where the music was coming from. I laughed thinking, *Is that Sal or is Arthur's phone somewhere around here?* I was running late and left without figuring it out.

After a tasty breakfast with family, I walked back to our house and went into Arthur's room to see how he was doing. He was just waking up and we began a conversation, when I noticed his cell phone, lying on his bedside dresser. I asked him if he had left it downstairs or if it was there all night on his dresser. He said it has been on his dresser all night. I laughed out loud again and told him what happened as I was putting my shoes on this morning at the bottom of the stairs. He smiled at me and we both laughed, saying to each other. "How does he do that?" And by the way, after a thorough house cleaning, nothing was ever found that could have made that mysterious tune!

A Fabulous Fragrance

I think a fragrance is all about sensations and imagery,
and can evoke visions, feelings and thoughts.

–Shakira, Singer, Songwriter, Actress

I'm getting close to finishing this book, but I have to add in a whole new way Sal has been showing up lately. It started so subtly that it literally snuck up on me. As I fall asleep and as I wake up; I have been noticing that I smell heavenly divine scents that I can't seem to recognize or figure out where they are coming from. I just brushed it off thinking it must be an essential oil or a lotion I had used. But it kept happening and I began to really notice if I did use an oil or lotion, but no I did not burn a candle or use any kind of fragrance that would produce this intoxicating fragrance and then I only smelled it at bedtime and upon awakening. And whether I was home or away this fragrance would permeate my atmosphere. I laughed knowing it was Sal, because I can now also feel his high vibe and recognize it.

Also, something happened about a week before the fragrance episodes started enhancing my life; that may have something to do with this. I have a special white T-shirt of Sal's that I took from his room after he passed. I kept this soft white V-neck undershirt in my pajama drawer, because it smelled of Sal. Every person has their own smell; this shirt had Sal's scent. But it also carried the cologne that Sal liked to wear, another good fragrance. Recently, I realized I needed to wash this T-shirt. I knew the smells had faded over the past five years and it really did not carry the Sal scent anymore. I also realized the uncanny connection between these two events. Giving up my last connection on earth of the Sal scent and then falling asleep to a really wonderful fragrance that came out of nowhere. This "nowhere" scent was not the cologne he wore but more like an essential oil blend of scents that seem to engulf me in security and comfort.

But of course, by now, Sal knows I need validation for every miracle he sends me. So … he started pulling in others into the scent miracle, so I wouldn't think my nose was playing tricks on me. This year on November 25th, the sixth-year anniversary of his transition, my friend Gail was visiting from Kauai and was staying with me. I knew the 25th was going to be a hard day for me and I was happy she would be with me. She knew Sal and I well and has been a major support in my life. After my early morning meditation, I went downstairs into the kitchen where I could hear she was playing some soulful chants I had never heard before. As I walked down the stairs I could smell an uplifting scent that permeated the whole house. We had tea, talked, and listened to the new artist sing, as we were enjoying the sacred aroma that filled our lungs and hearts. It was getting to be late morning and as I started heading up the steps; I yelled back, "Oh, I love that incense, what is it?" Gail replied, "I love it too, I thought you were burning it!" We both laughed, knowing exactly where it was coming from and who was behind it.

About three week later, I had another houseguest come and stay in Sal's room. The room was ready, as I had cleaned and changed the sheets the day Gail left. My friend, Nancy brought her suitcase up to the bedroom and then joined me in the kitchen for some tea. She thanked me for the hospitality and then said, "And the room smells so good!" Again, no one had stayed in the room for three weeks and there is nothing in that room that smells at all. In fact I had been away for part of those three weeks and had the door closed and I did not go in there. I just laughed to myself and smiled. When the topic came up again the next day, I told her about the mysterious scents. Not only was this validation once again for me as I continue to get these delicious scents on some mornings and some nights, but it was a long awaited sign from Sal to Nancy. Nancy and Sal were mutual admirers of each other and there was an authentic love for one another. Nancy is a dear longtime friend from high school and witnessed Sal's life as he grew into the amazing young man he was when he made his transition. Nancy kept telling me that she wanted a sign from Sal but she never gets them. I think Sal found a way to reach her without her inner critic interfering. She had no reason to doubt that her senses were deceiving her because she just thought I had used a room spray or did something of that sort to make the room smell "so good!" Without the doubting mind involved, she was able to get a clear sign from Sal.

Just the other day I got in the car to go out with a different friend, and she said, "Wow you smell good!" Again I had not put anything on and had been on a walk, so if anything I might smell sweaty! I laughed to myself and knew where the good smell was coming from. I love this new sign, because others are enjoying it as well, and it is an easy and fun way for Sal to let me know he is near, as it happens often now.

A Heavenly Massage

When we choose not to focus on what is missing from our lives but are grateful for the abundance that's present ... we experience heaven on earth.

–SARAH BAN BREATHNACH, AUTHOR

After Sal's transition I was getting massages often. Many of my students and friends were gifting me massages after Sal's passing. I found that during the massage session, I would immediately go into a very deep place throughout the entire massage. The relaxation of the body also helped relax my mind and allowed me to let go of emotional and mental resistance and trauma. I was able to drift in and out of different levels of consciousness, including sleep. Yet I would remain conscious throughout the massage. From my training in yoga nidra, a sleep based form of meditation, I knew the slower brain waves of theta and delta were very healing for me and I had practice staying conscious during these states.

I had several very powerful experiences that happened during the massage sessions. During one particular massage I felt the presence of Sal very strong. I entered a very deep place of unconditional love. The feeling of the love was so intense that it was almost overwhelming. This feeling of love just swept over me and engulfed me. I was engulfed in a deep inner peace and all worldly concerns faded away, I was so present in this intense feeling of being loved and of loving. Nothing existed for me but this deeply nurturing feeling of what I can only describe as unconditional love.

Tears were streaming down my checks, because of the intense love I was feeling. It was beautiful and was not of this world. It felt as though Sal took me by the hand and led me to this place of powerful, unconditional love. I felt him conveying to me that this is where he is now; it is a place we on earth, call heaven. He told me that I do not have to wait until I die to experience this, that I could experience this feeling of huge love now, on earth. This experience has been a wonderful gift in my life and gives me something to aspire to that is real. I have felt this many times since in meditation. Especially when I focus my mind on my love for Sal and Arthur and other family and friends who I love so much. The more we place our attention on this unconditional love, the more it shows up in our lives. And the more we begin to love ourselves and realize that in our true essence, we are all pure, unconditional love.

To hold love in our hearts, no matter what the outside circumstances are, is true *unconditional* love. Feeling love no matter what life brings is the true meaning of unconditional love. And how can we do this? By staying in the present moment. By being aware of what we are thinking and how we are feeling. The first step is awareness, and the second is to stay in the present moment. In Part III, I give practical steps on how to stay present and build your presence power.

Message from a Baci Candy

The precise location of heaven on earth has never been established but it may very well be right here."

–Herb Caen, Journalist for the San Francisco Chronicle

I was in Carmel with my sisters and nieces and nephews. They were having fun carousing the unique shops, while I was off on my own to run an errand. While I was waiting to meet up with them, I decided to have a late afternoon hot tea and chocolate break, one of my favorite things to do for an afternoon boost. I often teach a meditation class titled, *Dark Chocolate and Hot Tea.* In the class we slowly and mindfully, unwrap the chocolate, smell it first, and slowly let it melt in our mouths as we sip on the hot tea. We focus on the warmth of the hot tea going down our throat and focus on the taste of the chocolate and tea, etc. It is a delightful practice in mindfulness and presence.

I was sitting outside by myself at a table in front of a small, quaint, old-fashioned grocery store, Neilson's Grocery. I was mindfully enjoying the aroma of the tea as I slowly sipped it, fully aware of the warm sensation flowing down my throat as I swallowed it, enjoying the impactful flavor of the herbs. I bought one Baci chocolate to savor with my tea. I call Baci candies, the Italian kisses. Baci in Italian translates to kiss. They are a chocolate candy with a hazelnut on the inside, you can find these candies all over Italy. I was now dipping the Baci in the hot tea and very slowly savoring the melted chocolate in my mouth. I could also feel the heat of the sunrays beating on my back; the warmth relaxed my neck, shoulders, and upper back muscles. As I was in a meditative state of ecstasy, I remembered what Sal told me on the massage table about being in that place of pure positive energy and unconditional love. He told me that I could be in that place here on earth. I began to realize that heaven is a state of mind and not a place. And it is a choice we make to be in that state, not a place we must find. Sal not only told me but also showed me that heaven can be right here, right now. All we really need to do is let go of all our resistance and fear and allow the peace of the present moment in. And for that wonderful moment I got it and I felt it. I knew there was no barrier between Sal and I, he was closer than close. He was here with me as I savored my hot tea and delicious Baci.

I decided to read my message from the Baci candy. Each Baci candy comes with a message inside, like a fortunate cookie. It is written in Italian, Spanish, French, and English. I was blown away when I read my Baci message. It read: *Have you come down from Heaven or am I in heaven too?*

Whoa! Again, what are the chances I am going to get a message from a Baci chocolate about exactly what I was thinking about? Usually their messages are romantic and not about heaven!

I was once again getting validation from the universe and a fun message from Sal, saying: *Hey I am right here with you, when you tuned in.* The simple act of being present makes life so much more enjoyable!

Partiers Can Be Enlightened

It's all about love and how we are all connected

–MARK WAHLBERG, ACTOR

Journal Notes: January 4, 2015

The other day I cleaned out the smart car and washed it. (The smart car was Sal's car.) It was a beautiful sunny day in Pacific Grove where I was doing some work, but since it was Sunday, I decided to take a break and drive to Big Sur, in the smart car. I rolled down the convertible top and began driving on the winding road to Big Sur. The sky was bright blue, as were the crashing waves below as I drove over the fabulous Bixby Bridge. I was feeling free and easy with the heater on and the top down, breathing in the refreshing sea air.

The night before, I had thought of how I had been connecting with Sal and how he had become my direct line to the Infinite Intelligence. I asked Source if this was ok, after all, Sal was a partier as most twenty-four-year-olds are. He was a casual partier, in fact he went for months at time without drinking or going to parties. But he was living in San Francisco and he was a social young man.

Although, I knew him from a seed in my womb and knew he was pure goodness, a soul acting the earth role he had chosen. But it was just a quick thought that entered my mind, and I thought; I wonder if this is alright? (Of course, I knew it was alright, but that doubting inner critic popped up, and we hear it when we are aware of our own thoughts.) For the past year since Sal passed, I was using my intense love for Sal as a direct line to Source, as well as communing with Sal. So in response to my question, I got an unexpected reply; Source and Sal, definitely have a sense of humor!

I turned on the radio, invigorated because I could feel Sal's and Arthur's fun energy with me and I knew I was tuning into a station that both Sal and Arthur listened to. Arthur had been driving this car most of the time since Sal passed. A rap song came on that I have never heard before or since. The song went something like this:

Jesus was a partier and partied all night
Krishna was a partier and partied all night
Buddha was a partier and partied all night, etc.

I was literally in shock and laughing out loud!

I have never heard this song again and I'm not even sure where it came from!

Wow! Funny, amazing, and divine timing!

A Random Chihuahua

Synchronicities are not flukes or random events—they're intentional reflections of our intuition working with the perfect order of all things in the unseen world.

–SONIA CHOQUETTE, AUTHOR

Journal Notes: July 12, 2014 (I wrote this entry while staying in Pacific Grove).

It has been eight months since Sal left. This is probably the worst I have felt since he left. And this depressed feeling has lasted over twenty-four hours. I have not been able to get myself out of this funk. I decided to go to one of the most gorgeous beaches in the world, Carmel Ocean Beach. It is one of the few beaches where they allow dogs to romp freely. And with the help of Doris Day, dogs in Carmel have more freedom than in most places. The local folk in Carmel have some of the most playful and interesting dogs. I was hoping that being around the unconditional love that almost all dogs exude and the fresh cool air of the beach would help lift my spirits. I love the sound of the waves crashing on the beach, and this beach has the most pristine fine white sand, which feels heavenly on bare feet and in between the toes.

I have come to realize that our environment is stronger than our will. So placing ourselves in an environment that opens our hearts and is special to us can help our mood tremendously. So I headed to Carmel beach; I walked for only a short time before I sat down on the warm, soft, white sand. When sadness hits, it can really drain the life force right out of us. I felt tired so I decided to just sit. I closed my eyes and did my best to just stopped thinking and become present. I focused on my breath. I felt the cool air come in through my nostrils and go out a little bit warmer. I began to breathe deep and very slowly. I enjoyed the familiar scent of the kelp and salt air of the seaside. I felt the cool ocean breeze on my face and at the same time I felt the warm sun on my face. The contrast of the cool air and warm sun felt delicious.

I looked right into the bright sun with closed eyes. So I could see the light through my eyelids. I felt myself begin to relax and just let go of tension, all tension—mental, emotional, and physical. I guided myself into the silence and I let go. After only a few minutes of this, a small puppy came running right up to me and interrupted my meditation. The adorable puppy without hesitation jumped into my lap and started excitedly giving me little puppy kisses on my checks. This little dog looked exactly like Sal's dog that he shared with his girlfriend, Lauren. Bella was now living with Lauren and her mom. A young man just about the same age as Sal came running up calling the dog to come back to him. He shouted Bella, Bella! As I began to tell him that my son had a dog with the same exact name and looked almost identical to this dog, I realized this was Sal's way of reaching out to me. Letting me know, he (his essence) did not leave.

Not only did this dog look exactly like Bella, it had the same disposition and it had the same name and the owner was a young man around Sal's age. Sal probably would have never picked out a Chihuahua as his dream dog, but he rescued Bella. If he did not rescue her she most likely would have died at the ranch where he rescued her. He gave her as a gift to Lauren but she could not take Bella at that time, so Sal kept Bella and fell in love with her. He took her everywhere he went. I meet Sal weekly in San Francisco for dinner, where he lived and attended college. We always had to sit outside under heat lamps so Bella could come out with us.

When I was dropped down in sorrow, Sal could not reach me until I stopped all the noisy, chaotic thoughts in my head. Until I let go of the fear that had a tight grip on me. When I simply moved to just "being" by just quieting my mind by focusing on my breath he was able to come through. And I was also able to be open to receive him when I let go of fear and moved into presence. He could not physically soothe me so he set this random Bella to jump into my arms and give me little licks of love.

Later when I went home to my apartment and was cooking dinner, I had an insight; it was that our greatest responsibility as human beings is our state of consciousness. Our state of consciousness in the present moment, affects not only our next moment but also our future. Our state of consciousness not only affects our future but it ripples out from us into the matrix that holds us all together. Our state of mind affects all those around us. Are we polluting the environment around us, or are we bringing in joy and peace to the environment around us?

I felt a shift in me, when I remembered this great truth. I snapped out of my self-doubting, sad mood. I shifted my thoughts to gratitude, staying present, and focused on enjoying this special time I have to be alone and relax. I remembered that Sal and Source have my back!

Sal Shops

*The best and most beautiful things in the world cannot be seen
or even touched - they must be felt with the heart.*

–HELEN KELLER

Several months after Sal passed, my older sisters, Geri and Sally thought it would be good for the three of us to take a trip together. We went on a trip to Peru and Argentina. Our dear friend, Angela, grew up in Peru and still has family and an apartment there. She generously offered to come and we stayed at her apartment and visited with her family. Our last night of the trip, we ate dinner at the outdoor mall across the street from Angela's apartment in Lima. As we were leaving, I saw this interesting store and was intuitively drawn in for a quick look. We were leaving for the airport that night so there wasn't much time. I loved everything in this store. I bought a purse, but the funny thing is I felt Sal so strong with me in this store. It felt as though he led me to this store and he was encouraging me to buy this purse. Just looking at this purse made me feel happy. A few days after I got home I noticed that this purse had fun, hidden messages on it. They were embroidered in gold threads on the purse. The purse is made of a thick cotton fabric, which is bright and colorful. So the embroidery is hard to see at first glance. The messages on the purse are the very messages that Sal has been telling me! One message says, *you are loved*, another says, *we are one*! Another funny thing is that even though the designer's name is Desigual, the zipper of the purse, has a charm attached to it with the letter S! S for Sal? Why not D for Desigual?

More coincidences or am I learning to play and align with Sal? Are we bridging heaven and earth? Are we connecting from the nonphysical and the physical? Is our consciousness blending beyond the borders of form and the formless realm? I cannot answer all of these questions, but what I know for sure is that I experience a strong playfulness with Sal when I stay present and relaxed in my life.

There are many fun stories to tell about shopping with Sal. But I will tell just one more. I was in northern Washington, out in the middle of nowhere. We had a family project developing there. The situation was feeling very bleak and not going well.

I decided to clear my mind and take a drive to a quaint town, which was about an hour away. I ran into a unique clothing shop there and thought maybe a little retail therapy might be good for the soul! I was looking around, but wasn't really seeing anything I could afford or even wanted to buy. In the back of the store there was a little basket filled with discounted items. Rolled up in a little ball was a pretty white cotton blouse with blue embroidered butterflies on it! Of course, blue butteries are my strongest sign from Sal. But, this is only the beginning of the fun. I noticed the designer is Desigual! Not one other item in this entire store was from Desigual. And it was 50% off! Desigual seems to be the store and brand that Sal likes to play with.

I happily took the butterfly blouse up to the register as I was silently thanking Sal for the deep discount. But then, the lovely woman behind the counter told me that it was actually 75% off! I had no idea how or why it was 75% off, but I didn't question it and just laughed out loud, knowing Sal was working his magic. But then... the cost was $12.12, his birth date!

As usual he is over the top with his creative fun from the formless realm. But, what was most important was that in a time when I was feeling stuck, he was making me laugh and validating that he is still here, only invisible

Mediums

When you stop existing and you start truly living, each moment of the day comes alive with wonderment and synchronicity.

—STEVE MARABOLI, AUTHOR

On a Saturday afternoon, my friend Hilary and I decided to attend a lecture at the Center for Spiritual Awakening. This center is only a few blocks away from where we were staying. The topic of the lecture was, "Forever Connected." I liked the topic as it was something I was experiencing. But to my surprise the speaker was a medium. I had such a good connection with Sal that I never sought a medium. But this was a group medium lecture. There were maybe two hundred people or more in the lecture. The medium, Deb Shepard, was very good. Spirits were coming through and she was successfully connecting them with their loved ones.

What I witnessed from the audience was so beautiful. Most of these people seemed unsure if there is life beyond our physical life on earth. The medium acted as a liaison between the passed persons and their loved ones here on earth. The family and friends were astonished, and tears would begin to flow as they realized that somehow their loved ones were still alive.

After the intermission, we went back to our seats; I immediately felt Sal! I turned to Hilary and said, "He's here, I feel him." No sooner had I said that to Hilary, the medium began describing Sal. I stood up and told her she was describing my son. It was all accurate, Sal spoke of how he and I have a very strong bond and how unusual this is. He said that I handled death very different than most. He described in detail that I have an electric candle by his portrait that never goes out. How we celebrate his birthday every year with his friends and family. All of this is true. It confirmed what I already knew; our loved ones are still interested in our lives and in growing our relationship and love for one another. None of the other spirits that came through said anything like what Sal said about us and about me.

But the biggest surprise was that my brother Michael was with Sal! She said there is another young man here with Sal. "He is showing me that his death was caused by something around the head." She demonstrated what Michael was showing her, by moving her hands around her head. As you know from Part I, Michael was killed by several kicks, all to the head. That made it clear to me that it was Michael. But the best part of all this was the last thing she picked up on.

She said there is a dog with them—a big dog; for a moment I forgot about Michael's best friend, his dog Angus. Michael and Angus were rarely apart. When she said it is a Rottweiler, it blew me away, because that is the breed that Angus was, or should I say is! She quickly moved on to the next spirit coming through as she was trying to reach as many as possible in this lecture.

It is interesting that earlier in the day, Choosing Hope, the short story I had written about Michael in 1993, was on my desk, as I had been working on this book. Hilary knew I had a brother who had been murdered, but never knew any details about it. Hilary read it and was moved by the short story, she had some questions and we discussed it over our morning tea. So just that morning we were talking about Michael and here he was coming through a few hours later through a medium.

I do believe that an authentic medium can make all the difference to mourning humans left here on earth after their loved ones have made their transition. There is a foundation called *Forever Family* that helps people with this process. They have certified mediums and have a list they recommend. It personally helped the founders of *Forever Family*, a couple that had lost their daughter, so they have made it their life purpose to help others find the connection to their loved ones through mediums, as they did.

The Precious and Precocious Birthday Song

The purpose of synchronicity is to release the riches of the spiritual Self.

–DAVID RICHO, PhD, AUTHOR, PSYCHOTHERAPIST

One year I received the best birthday present ever. Sal loved music and made beats and wrote lyrics. He composed a song for my birthday. He was barely sixteen at the time and Arthur was thirteen. Sal was playing football at the time and commuting to San Francisco, a forty-five-minute drive without traffic. That alone was like a full-time job with practices twice a day. He would leave for football practice at 5 a.m. and get home at 6:30 p.m., eat dinner and do his homework. So between school, homework, and football, he had very little time, not to mention that my birthday is during finals and four days after his own. But he managed to write me the most personal and precious song. And he got Arthur involved as well. He knew it would be extra special for me if Arthur wrote and sang part of the song too. I loved that both of them worked together so well, and I love what each one wrote for me in their own unique way.

This was one of Sal's early songs so he took the beat from Tupac's, *Dear Mama*. Sal and Arthur surprised me with the song on my birthday night after the family went out for dinner with some friends. We came home for some birthday cake and to open presents and that's when they played my song. My heart melted with such love and gratitude! At that time what was so special about the song was the sweetness in Arthur's voice and the strong emotion in Sal's voice, especially as he sang the chorus.

But what I realized after Sal's passing was that this very song was written for me after he passed. Why do I say that? These are the words of what he called the hook, also known as the chorus:

Mom promise me you'll never pout, when it comes to us there is no doubt, cuz we'll be together, as long as forever, Being best pals like Cheech and Chong, From the bottom of my heart I love you mom and that's why I wrote this song.

First of all, I am naturally a cheerful and optimistic person most of the time. I don't think Sal ever once saw me pout. And in the song, pout doesn't have a rhyming partner to make it a word he just threw in. But I might be prone to pouting if he leaves the planet!

In the birthday song, eight years before Sal made his transition, he tells me, we'll be TOGETHER FOREVER, hence the title of this book. This is how he words it: *we'll be together for as long as forever*. It was like he was saying don't pout when I pass cuz we'll be together throughout eternity, for as long as forever. He also reassures me by saying, "when it comes to us there is no *doubt*, cuz we'll be together as long as forever." And then he lets me know that we are best friends now and forever. And to top it all off he reassures me that he loves me from the bottom of his heart.

There are so many blessings associated with this song, but the greatest is I can still hear Sal in his own voice singing out loud to me how much he loves me, all the great things he sees in me, and that we will always be together! What a priceless gift. And how did he know? His soul certainly knew that the song would always put a smile on my face, cheer me up when I need it and get me higher when I am already feeling great.

Two days after Sal passed, I drove to the redwood forest for a walk. It was the first time I was alone since Sal's accident. This has already been spoken of in Part I. I was not sure I could handle hearing his voice and the song so early after his accident, but I put it on anyway. I waited until I got to the parking lot at the trailhead, before playing the song. As expected, I burst into tears and thought I might have actually died right there of a broken heart. Yet at the same time, hearing the words and his voice was comforting. I felt both the gratitude and the broken heart resided within me as I stepped out of the car and started my journey into the woods.

Here is the entire song.

Mom's Birthday Song by Sal and Arthur (2005)

Arthur: Happy birthday mom.

Sal: Happy birthday mom.
This song's for you, from me and Arthur

Arthur: Dear mom it's your birthday and you still look young,
you bring light to my days even brighter than the sun,
let's admit now that you're the best mom,
sorry I lied but I'm a brand new man so get down to my vibe,
I gotta tell you I'm your biggest fan,
you work too hard, now you gotta keep it real, pop a chill pill, you're on Arthur time,
now listen to my brother Sal drop a rhyme.

Sal (chorus):
Mom promise me you'll never pout,
when it comes to us there is no doubt,

cuz we'll be together, as long as forever,
Being best pals like Cheech and Chong,
From the bottom of my heart I love you mom and that's why I wrote
this song.

Sal: Our love is of the unbreakable type,
when we pass you know they looking at us, looking at us cuz
they're jealous.
Our connection is a once in a lifetime event, households like this they
ain't for rent,
so Mom it's your birthday!
Relax your mind, sip on some wine, and just listen to me rhyme.

Sal (chorus):

Arthur: Mom you truly are the coolest,
and there is no doubt in my mind my love for you is the fullest,
I appreciate everything you do,
sometimes I act a fool, and somehow you keep it cool,
when I'm scared I jump to you like a kangaroo,
so mom keep doing what you're doing, this here song is dedicated to you.

Sal (chorus):

Sal: The years have gone by and mom you still look fly,
never a dull moment as long as you nearby,
growing up without you would be like eating ice cream with a fork,
if I just had dad I might have been a dork.
Mom you got the cool side of cool,
and the smart side of smart,
and everything in between,
you'll always be my Italiano queen,
mom I'm sorry for that trouble that I got in,
you were the one that said it was just a phase,
got in trouble one more time you still found the good out of bad,
happened again
and now I know through thick and thin you'll always be my friend,

now that's something,
true love never ends!

Sal (chorus):

Sal: Some moms are nice, some moms are cool,
some moms cook rice, some moms cook stew,
Mom you're the best, you put the other moms to test,
and you gonna wanna trust me on this.
I don't know what I'd do without you, in my life,
you taught me not to tell them lies, how you so damn wise!
5 foot 4, but you a person super-sized!
When I think I got no one you're right by my side,
when I think I got no one you're down to ride,
when I think there is no answer you give me the solution,
your so special, you're defogging the world's pollution.
How you know all this stuff,
you seem like you can do anything,
you're so damn tough,
I can never appreciate you enough,
and I know you'll love me no matter what,
even when the alcohol cabinet was raided (chuckles),
I'm here to say mom, you are appreciated!

Saint Michael Gives Me Validation

It is presumptuous in me to wish to choose my path,
because I cannot tell which path is best for me. I must leave to God,
who knows what path is best for me.

−TERESA OF ÁVILA

Being raised Catholic, I have always felt a connection to angels. It was one
of the things the nun's taught us that rang true to me and that proved to
be true in my experience, as long as I could remember. I know there is an
invisible force we call angels and that many people tap into this force for

guidance and protection and have miraculous stories to tell. I love playing with angel cards and found them to be helpful for friends, family, and
myself. Angel cards are also a good way to strengthen your own intuition.

One day, about two months after Sal made his transition, I notice
my deck of angel cards in a drawer. This particular deck of angel cards was
only for St Michael, the archangel. St Michael is an angel one prays to for
protection. Everyone who is raised Catholic knows about Saint Michael,
the Archangel, and that he is a fierce protector.

When Sal and Arthur were teenagers and out with their friends I
would always call on Saint Michael to watch over them. So when I came
across this deck of cards, I held the deck in my hands and asked Saint
Michael why he couldn't protect Sal that night on the motorcycle. I took
the cards out of the box and held them in my hands facedown. I mixed
them up as I asked St. Michael again, "Why couldn't you protect Sal?" I
already knew the answer. I knew there was a divine order to the universe
and that we cannot always understand why things happen to us, at least
not right away, and sometimes not at all. I knew our sacred contract was in
order and that Sal's soul had chosen to leave his body. But I did it anyway;
curious as to what would come up. I always like more validation! I slowly
picked only one card from the deck. I picked a card I have never seen in
this deck before, and I have played with this deck many times before. It was
probably the only card in the whole deck that would make any sense for
this particular question. The card read, "God is in charge." Once again the
angels had answered me in simple direct language!

CHAPTER SEVEN:

Signs From Sal to Family and Friends

The way I see it, there are just two things we need to know: The universe has our back. Everything is going to turn out okay.

–PAM GROUT, AUTHOR

By Arthur Enea O'Brien, Sal's brother

I got up early on the day of Nov 15, 2014. It was the day the PlayStation 4 (PS4) had just been released, and I wanted to get to the store early to beat the lines. I swiftly threw on my clothes and rushed out the door. As I stepped out onto the back patio, I felt the brisk, cold air hit my face. I decided it wasn't top down smart car weather. I hopped into Sal's smart car and headed over to Gamespot, which was about a fifteen-minute drive from my house. As I was pulling into the parking lot, I saw people leaving the store with PS4s in their hands. I parked and speedily made my way toward the store. I got in and was relieved to see that there was no line. After successfully purchasing the PS4 and feeling happy that I had beaten the lines, I gallantly walked back to the smart car, in a state of momentary bliss. And by momentary I really do mean a moment. As soon as I got into the smart car, I realized I couldn't find the keys anywhere. I started searching around the car like an artic fox searching for it's prey. Shoving my head under the seats, unsuccessfully extending my arm into crevices like they were made of elastic, but to no avail. As soon as I was starting to give up and was thinking of heading back into the store to explain my embarrassing predicament, the keys suddenly just fell from the ceiling of my car, right onto my lap. It honestly didn't make much sense as I do not recall leaving them in the sun visor (which I have never done before) and I certainly didn't tape them to the ceiling of the smart car. I internally thanked Sal for taking care of me once again, and headed back home.

I've had countless dreams about Sal since he has passed. And every single one of them has been great and worthy of telling. One dream however has stood out to me more than all the others. In most of my dreams Sal comes to me as his younger self, with short hair, not the longer hair he sported in his later years. I can't explain why, but that's usually how he looks in my dreams. In this one particular dream I had of him, soon after he passed, he did have his longer hair. It was a simple dream, yet it meant so much to me. In my dream I was sitting down on our couch watching Netflix, when Sal came over and sat down next to me. We talked and laughed for hours. Made fun of the TV shows we were watching like usual. It was like he had never passed and it was just another day. It reminded me of how well we got along, even if we were just sitting around watching TV. There are no words to describe how lucky and appreciative I am to be his little brother. I still dream of him often, and hope that never changes.

By Kelsey Guntren, Sal's Friend

I am fortunate enough to have met Sal in middle school. We shared the same friend group, but it wasn't until high school that he became one of my best friends and we remained extremely close through college and after. Through our life challenges, teenage-related dilemmas, achievements, and despair we were there for each other. I strongly guard and cherish the memories that we shared together, especially now that he is no longer physically here. In some ways, I feel that Sal is indescribable. His presence was incredibly powerful. He was vibrant, energetic, and enthusiastic. However, he had this calm and encouraging side to him, an understanding about him that would tap into your emotions to ensure you were okay. His larger-than-life attitude made him attract people from all walks of life. There was nothing that could hold him down. Although his passing devastated me, I quickly understood he is very much with me every day.

When Sal died it didn't take long for him to comfort me through nature—a bird or a rainbow in times that I needed him the most. One of the most validating experiences that Sal showed me he is still here was through a psychic medium. It was five years after Sal died that I went to see the medium. Sal came through strong, dancing and laughing. The medium described him as a risk-taker with a loving heart and positive energy. The medium said that Sal told people that he felt like he wasn't going to live till he was old. This was true as I found out he told multiple people that he was going to die young. This is one of the reasons I believe that Sal lived such a loving and vivacious life. Sal validated that his family and friends celebrate him yearly, which is true because every year on Sal's birthday a large group of us gather to remember Sal, share memories, and reflect on Sal's light and ability to bring people together. At one point the medium said that Sal was joking that his picture was greater than God. I didn't understand this at first until I spoke to Annie (Sal's mom) as soon as I got out of the reading.

After Sal died, his friends and family came together to build a yurt in his memory. It is in the most beautiful location along the mountains where anyone can go to pray, meditate, and be close to Sal. It is called Sal's Sanctuary of Peace. There is an altar that displays pictures of a few of the world's spiritual leaders in eight by ten frames. However, the picture of Sal next to these spiritual leaders is larger. Annie was asked if she could get a smaller photo of Sal because someone that visited the sanctuary thought it wasn't right that Sal's photo was bigger than the enlightened Masters of the world whose photos were also in the sanctuary. It was hilarious that he recognized this and really made us laugh. Making fun of the human ego and the little things that can cause drama in our lives. Making Sal's photo smaller is never going to change the presence Sal emits in the sanctuary. These great masters would never care what size Sal's photo is in comparison to theirs. They probably all got a good laugh from it as Sal joked about it to the medium.

I miss Sal physically being here, but I am comforted in knowing that I can still talk to him and that he never truly left.

By Lauren Ward, Sal's Girlfriend

As I begin to write my memories of the one true element that connects my soul to Sal's soul, I find myself flooded with emotions of sadness and disbelief, but also with gratitude and unconditional love.

Before I explain the first day I was gifted by a rainbow, I'd like to briefly share about Bella and why she meant the world to both Sal and I. Bella was our dog, but if you asked those close to us she was more than just an animal, she was unconditional love and spent most of her life side by side with one of us. When I wasn't around, Sal and Bella spent day in and day out together. Sharing a seat in the car, a jacket on the motorcycle, and a bed at night. Bella was truly our little blessing and played a significant role in our everyday happiness.

After Sal made his transition, Bella and her physical presence was the one thing that kept me closest to Sal through the healing of his passing.

I'd now like to begin to my rainbow experience.

The beginning of my rainbow experiences started about forty-eight hours after Sal made his transformation from the form to the formless. I remember this day as if it were yesterday. As I sat in my grandmothers living room rocking chair, Bella in my lap, the Raiders' blanket, I made Sal five years prior, wrapped around us, blinds closed from the sunlight and my loved ones sitting on the couch next to me. We all sat quietly and were still in shock. As I sat there feeling hopeless, lost, weak, and uncertain, I happened to look down at my feet. I couldn't believe my eyes; two strips of rainbows about an inch in diameter and three inches in length were highlighted over the tops of my feet in bright vivid colors. If it wasn't for my family, also sitting in the room, I'm not sure people would believe me when I said the blinds were closed and that rainbows still somehow appeared. It wasn't until later that I learned from Sal's mother that rainbows are the highest meditative level. That he has made his transformation and has chosen to present his soul to me by using light.

I'll never forget the feeling of seeing these rainbows, I felt his presence very strongly with me. I felt he was saying, "I am here. I am right here." I felt him right here on earth with me. After receiving my rainbows, I was finally able to eat food and get some sleep. I had for the first time believed in something considered a "higher power." I have no doubt that this was Sal's way of showing me he is okay and to attempt to heal me, as the rainbows brought a peace and a calmness with them. They stayed on my feet for an entire hour working their magic on healing me. However, the healing continues even now. This loss is not something you can get over, but rather continues through the years that pass. But with these miracle-healing rainbows, Sal gave me something physical right away to let me know he is here with me and always will be.

I could probably spend an entire day writing about my rainbow experiences. Never in my life had I believed in the afterlife, and that there is NO death until I survived losing my best friend. The rainbows took me from a dark place of grief and despair to a place of hope, light, and love. Though the rainbows cannot take away the pain of losing a loved one, I find peace knowing he's never too far and that even the darkest moments have a light if you stay open and don't miss opportunities to find it.

Another rainbow experience I would like to share is the day Sal's family and I spread some of his ashes in Clear Lake. One of his favorite places to get away and the first place he taught me to wake surf. Sal and several of his close friends had a beautiful home they rented on the lakeside in Clear Lake. It was always his dream to have a home on a lake and wakeboard with family and friends to his hearts delight. At the young age of just twenty-four, Sal attained this dream.

It's an interesting feeling when you go somewhere you used to go with that person and now you are there to celebrate that person's life. Then you realize they aren't there ... In moments of celebration, come moments of sadness but even in those moments Sal has never failed to show me we are never apart.

On the afternoon we decided to spread some of Sal's ashes in Clear Lake, mine and Sal's friends, and his family took his boat out on the lake. We played some of Sal's favorite music, sipped on some of his favorite Blue

Label whiskey, and took in these moments I would hold closest to my heart and soul forever.

As we pulled away from the dock, it started to rain, we couldn't believe it! Not rain! We're on a boat! But as we continued cruising down the lake, we found a little spot that had a little bit of sunshine where we could float, say our messages to Sal, and spread some ashes. After our sacred and intimate ceremony, we arrived at one of Sal's favorite lakeside bar and restaurants. When we got onto the dock ... as we were now on land and walking toward the restaurant, we notice a HUGE DOUBLE RAINBOW IN THE SKY! Not one, but TWO vivid, bright rainbows appeared over us as we stood on the dock... (deep breath). This double rainbow appeared right over Sal's house in Clear Lake that he shared so many good times with his family and friends. Again, to my disbelief, Sal was once again with us. Shining through the light and gracing us with his presence. Though my heart was heavy for celebrating his beautiful life without him, the rainbow above, for everyone to see, was once again proof that nothing can break unconditional love and when you are open to receive, they will be with you.

I thank Sal most days for gifting me with the light to see my rainbows. These are just two of the unknown number (too many to count) I have experienced over the past seven years. Truth is, without them. I would not be the person I am today. Still filled with hope, love & light.

Immense gratitude for my angel.

By Dustin Berkowitz, Sal's Close Friend and Roommate

Sal was one of my best friends and even though I didn't know him from childhood like many of his other friends, I had a very close bond with him and he was a big part of my life. We lived together in San Francisco, traveled together, and shared so many good memories.

About two days after Sal passed, I was in my room at the house we lived in together with his brother and a few other roommates; it was a large house. But no one was home, I was sitting in my room feeling so empty, lost, and sad. I was still in shock; it had all happened so suddenly. Sal was the glue that held many of us together; he was upbeat and a leader. As I sat there listening to his music, my heart ached and I felt so alone. When suddenly small round rainbows about an inch in diameter appeared on my hands and arms. They seemed to come out of nowhere, I never did figure out how these rainbows appeared. But when they came, I felt Sal's presence. The rainbows seemed to carry a message from Sal that I was not alone and that he was with me, right now. They stayed for about twenty minutes and I felt better. But this one time was only the beginning of so many rainbows in my life, and even to this day I still see rainbows, when I think of Sal or when I need a boost from life's difficulties.

Sal passed only three days before Thanksgiving. I woke up on Thanksgiving morning and immediately my thoughts went to Sal. I felt so bad for his family and I decided to decline my own family's dinner invite and bring a Thanksgiving dinner over to Sal's family's house. I knew they were not capable of putting together a Thanksgiving dinner. But I had no idea how I was going to find one this late either. But somehow it all worked out. I felt so guided by Sal. I went to a favorite neighborhood deli of Sal's and mine, near our home. By some miracle, there was only one turkey left! Then I went to several other places that had exactly what I needed to put together an incredible gourmet Thanksgiving dinner for Sal's family. We had a beautiful dinner around their dining room table. They had extended family there as well and the family was comforted by all the support and love flowing in. It was bittersweet, but on the sweet side, we all felt Sal, and went around the table saying what we were most grateful for about Sal. We all felt love and comfort in being together. Bitter in that it was so fresh and we all felt shocked and heartbroken.

Lately, I constantly see 12:12's everywhere; when I am trying to make a decision, a 12:12 will flash either on my phone or on a sign, or the license plate of the car in front of me. It is always a clue to guide me in the right direction. I feel Sal all the time. I never thought this was possible for me. I've learned from Sal, we don't die, we keep on going, and we stay connected with one another.

I'll never forget the beautiful double rainbow we saw right over our house in Clear Lake after we dispersed some of his ashes. It was huge, vivid, and carried Sal's presence once again. All of us saw this amazing rainbow and felt Sal's presence from it.

By Sally Enea Servidio Craig, Sal's Aunt

One morning I was out on my deck, which is on the Napa River, enjoying a cup of coffee. I was talking on the phone with my Sister, Anna Marie. She was asking if I had any signs from Sal. I said when we see rainbows, we say it's Sal, saying hello and think of him but I haven't had any other signs. AT THAT VERY MOMENT right after I said that, this hummingbird came up to me about a foot away from my face just fluttering and stayed there for about a minute! I told Anna Marie that maybe I'm getting a sign from Sal right now! That has never happened to me before and hasn't happened since. Just that once! Maybe it was Sal's great sense of humor.

After Sal passed, in many photos of Anna Marie, we would see light surrounding her, especially around her head. One time in particular it was really evident when we were in a beautiful amethyst cave in Argentina. This was only five months after Sal passed. Another time was when Anna Marie was leading her meditation and yoga retreat in Italy. It was only ten months after Sal passed. We were above Assisi in the area where St. Francis meditated and prayed. There were also some caves there. In the photos a bright white light appeared again around and above Anna Marie. They were group photos, but the light was always surrounding Anna Marie.

Sal Reaches People He Never Knew, But They Know Me

Many of my friends would call me and tell me they were talking about Sal and my connection with him when all of a sudden, they saw a definite sign from Sal. One friend was traveling in the car with others who know me. They were talking about all the signs I had been posting, when all of a sudden they passed a street sign with Sal's name on it. Another friend was talking to her husband about whether she should ask me if she can have a photo of Sal to paint. As she spoke of Sal, they passed a business with Sal's name on it. And many more such occurrences. Below is an example of these synchronistic occurrences.

From Geri Jones, My Friend and Student of Twenty-Seven Years

I have known Anna Marie Enea for many years now, as a yoga/meditation teacher and a dear friend. I maybe met her son Sal once briefly but didn't really know him. However, she spoke of him often, and I felt I knew him through her. After his passing, I had a couple of events where I really felt like he connected with me.

The first occurred shortly after he passed. I was in a gift shop, wanting to buy Anna Marie something meaningful that maybe could lift her spirits a bit. I walked around the gift shop several times, down every isle, but could not find a thing. So I asked Sal to guide me to something if it was meant to be. I immediately went down an isle that I had been down several times already and was drawn to a picture frame with a poem on it that I felt was just perfect! I had looked at those shelves several times but did not see this until I asked for Sal's help. I really felt like he guided me there, and I felt his presence near me. It's hard to explain since I didn't really know him, but he seemed to be there. I gave Anna Marie the frame with a picture of Sal in it, and she thought it was perfect!

On another occasion after his passing, when Anna Marie started teaching her classes again, I was getting ready to go to her meditation class when something amazing happened. I was thinking strongly of her and how grateful I was that she was back to teaching classes and that I had her in my life. I went to one of our cupboards to get my dog a biscuit before I left, and there was a small rainbow on the door of the white cupboard. I looked around and couldn't figure out where it was coming from. I put my hand in front of it and it didn't go away. After I opened the door and got the dog treats it was gone when I shut the door again. The amazing thing about this is that Sal had been communicating with his loved ones through rainbows since his passing. I feel that since I was strongly thinking of Anna Marie with love, somehow I drew him to me.

Another way he has communicated with loved ones is through blue butterflies. One day while paying bills, I once again was thinking strongly about Anna Marie with love and appreciation for all she has taught me about the spiritual path. I don't know why I was thinking about this while paying bills, but I was! I reached into a basket I have with a bunch of return address labels in it that have been sent by various charities. By chance (or not!), I happened to pick a page of address labels with blue butterflies on them! I hadn't been looking when I reached into the basket.

So, I feel that maybe when my thoughts were so strong about Anna Marie, it put me in the perfect vibration to receive these "messages." I'm grateful that I got them and grateful I'm able to share them.

PART III:

TRANSCENDENCE

CHAPTER EIGHT:

The Power of Presence and Acceptance

Happiness is beneficial for the body, but it is grief that develops the powers of the mind.

–MARCEL PROUST, FRENCH PHILOSOPHER AND AUTHOR

Without the practice of acceptance and presence I would never have handled Sal's transition as well as I did. I would not have moved into peace as soon as I did. And without my daily morning practice of meditation, yoga, gratitude, and walking in nature, practicing acceptance and presence would have been harder. However, you do not need these particular practices to bring acceptance and presence into your life. This is what worked for me, but it is not the only path to presence and acceptance.

Presence

Who you are cannot be defined through thinking or mental labels or definitions, because it's beyond that. It is the very sense of being, or presence, that is there when you become conscious of the present moment. In essence, you and what we call the present moment are, at the deepest level, one.

–ECKHART TOLLE, AUTHOR

I don't know of a more enlightened teacher on the planet today when it comes to living in presence and acceptance than Eckhart Tolle. In 1999, I was drawn to go to East West bookstore. It was about a forty-five-minute drive from my house to get there and it was a Friday evening. My husband at the time worked late hours and I had no one to leave my children with; I rarely left my children other than when I went to work. We did not have funds for babysitters, but mostly I didn't leave them because I loved being with my children. I found my children were my favorite people to hang out with. Sal was nine and Arthur was six. I had a friend who would leave her kids off at my house often and our children were very close, so luckily she was happy to take them.

I had no idea why I was so drawn to go to East West on that Friday night until sometime later when it all made sense. I just thought I needed a little break and East West bookstore is a wonderful place to be, with its expansive selection of fascinating books, clothing, music, crystals, and sometimes speakers. When I arrived, I asked the woman at the store counter who the speaker was; it was Eckhart Tolle. Nobody had heard of him yet, but one person browsing near us overheard us and had read his book, *The Power of Now*, and said it was excellent. However, the room where he would be speaking was quite small and it was about an hour before his presentation and it was sold out, as many of the talks at East West are. I met a woman in the store who invited me to dinner across the street; it sounded fun and I was hungry as it was dinnertime for me, so I decided to join her.

When I returned to the store to do some browsing, the person behind the counter told me that there was now an opening to see the speaker. I thought about it for a moment and decided to attend, so I bought a ticket for twenty dollars and entered the room where he had already started speaking. Immediately my inner critic chimed in: *What did you just waste twenty dollars on?* This man is speaking so slowly and in such a monotone, he looks hunched over on that little stool. My judgmental inner critic said all that before I even got to my seat. I ended up getting to sit quite close to Eckhart, which I later realized was a blessing. In less than one moment after sitting there I felt an incredible loving presence emanating from this unusual speaker. And as I started listening and taking in what he was saying, an incredible phenomenon occurred. I literally felt my mind expanding, I felt an energy moving outward beyond my body and I felt as though I understood everything. Why we are here, where we came from, and how to live in a way that would make life so much more enjoyable! Not all of it stayed with me, but the part about staying present did. I bought his book, met him, and thanked him, had a short conversation with him, and he signed my book. I ended up reading the book over and over for years. I bought it for all my close friends; most did not "get it" at that time. I taught classes on the book to my meditation students, even before Oprah did the first ever global webinar. Oprah had the intelligence and intuition to quickly recognize Eckhart, for the enlightened teacher he is. Her global webinar, the first in the world, was with Eckhart Tolle as her guest; the class was on his third book, *A New Earth* in 2008.

I have practiced presence extensively since that first encounter I had with Eckhart Tolle, back in 1999. I now know the reason I was guided to go to East West bookstore that Friday evening so long ago. It was to meet Eckhart Tolle and learn his transformative teachings on presence, acceptance, and awakening. My soul is always yearning to awaken in the game of life. Synchronicity is our soul's wisdom guiding us home. Without living in presence, I would have never been able to accept Sal's death the very evening he died, nor would I be able to move into a place of love and gratitude so quickly, if at all.

We hear about presence a lot these days, but what does it really mean? It may mean different things to different people, but the way I use the word presence, it simply means to be fully in this present moment. Presence is NOT when you are thinking and living in the past or the future. Presence is when you are living fully and intensely in the now, the present moment. Presence is when you go into what some call, the witness consciousness. Presence emerges from a higher dimension than regular consciousness. It is the spacious awareness and alert stillness behind the incessant thoughts. When you are present you are totally aware of the voice in the head. You are aware of your sense perceptions, such as the sounds around you, what you are seeing, smelling, and the way your body feels. You will notice the cool breeze caressing your body; in a restaurant, you will be aware of the hum of conversation; in the summer, you will notice the smell of freshly cut grass, when you walk outside you will hear the birds singing, and when you walk in the neighborhood you will smell the jasmine in bloom, and so on. And you will also feel an *aliveness* in your body and all around you. When you live in presence you will eventually have a quiet mind. The incessant thoughts will slow down and sometimes subside completely for short periods of time.

Presence will keep you aware and alert to your surroundings. When you are present, you are much more grounded than when the mind is wandering around in the past or the future. You will feel more vibrantly alive and alert but relaxed at the same time. When your mind is drifting from past to future and being bombarded with nonstop thoughts, you cannot help but be aware of yourself only as this body, you are absorbed in the incessant thoughts that are continuous in your head. You think that is who you are. You might even say, "What thoughts in my head?" Because you are so accustomed to that state that it has become normal for you to be totally *unaware* of your true essence behind all the noise in the mind. Sadly, your identification is only with your mind and your body, with no awareness of your true essence, which is the underlying consciousness that allows for everything to occur.

When the mind is constantly chattering inside, the quiet voice of intuition cannot be heard or realized.

When you have disengaged from identification with the thinker, and the constant stream of thoughts, you are present. When you are present, a Higher Intelligence emerges. This Higher Intelligence can be *felt* and then the *realization* comes in that you are a droplet of this Higher Intelligence, a droplet of God. Hence, the term Self-Realization in the East came about, meaning you have realized who you truly are, beyond this body and these thoughts. You realize there is no duality; you *are* yourself. It's not me and myself. To clarify, the present moment living leads you into living in your true Essence. When you live in the present moment, it allows the ego to soften and with practice even diminish. Presence allows the true Essence to emerge, as the quote in the beginning of this section states—You (your true Essence) and the present moment are one. The underlying Consciousness (Infinite Intelligence) becomes revealed through the present moment living. The present moment in reality is who we truly are.

Presence can be described as a state of being and feeling, rather than thinking and doing. However, you can do and think while present. Mindfulness can be a confusing word because we are talking about having a quiet, empty mind, not a full mind. But it is a common term used for living in the present moment. But for the reason mentioned above, I prefer to use the word presence in place of mindfulness.

You can be aware and present as you function in this physical world, realizing that you are not of this material world (you are more than your body), but you are in it and can function in it. You can also plan for the future if you need to while holding presence, as you plan you are doing it in the now. For example, there is a difference in being present while you book your flight for the future and when you are constantly yearning for a future moment. While yearning for a future moment, you are thinking of the future and not aware of what you are doing at this moment.

For example, whenever you space out and can't remember where you put your keys, your mind was someplace else when you placed your keys down, other than the present moment. It was in the past or in the future, it was not in this moment fully present, or you would be aware of where you placed your keys. I'm just using this as an example; we all do this from time to time. It's fine but the point is to notice that you were not present and that's how you forgot where you kept your keys. That awareness is the first step to becoming more present. So give yourself credit for the awareness that recognizes when you were lost in thought and not in the present moment.

But how does living in the present transcend grief? Much of grief is felt when we are living in the past. The dictionary defines grief as "painful regret." When you have had a tragic loss in your life, it is natural for your mind, the thinker, the voice in the head, to pull you into the past, into regret and sorrow. It is not necessary to dwell on the past when you lose a loved one. They are not in the past, they are only in the present. The past is not real now, it was only real when it was in the present. Now it is just a vague memory.

It is important and part of the healing process, especially early on, to get photos together of that person and talk about them and remember great stories from the past about them. Talk about them constantly with friends and family, if that is what your heart is leading you to do. Allow your passionate love to swell up fully in your heart and share it with others who also loved them. It is important to honor that person and share that honor with others. That is why a beautiful celebration of life is important for the family and friends of the deceased one. When it first happens and the sting of the loss is so painful, you definitely need to fully feel the pain of the loss. You need to initially grieve and let the pain go to the very core of your being, but you also need to *let it go* out of your body. Fully feel it and then release it. The importance of the release cannot be emphasized enough here.

You can do all this in the present. You do not need to dwell in the past and be absorbed by the grief. Most important to realize is that your loved one is actually in the present with you, in the here and now. And the present is the only place you can be with them, the only place they reside, and the only place to truly feel them as they are now. You can keep your relationship with them going in the present, not in the past. The only place where life is for us is in the present. The present is synonymous with Life. The past and future are not real, just as time itself is not real. Time is a manmade concept. On earth we need time to function in our world. But you don't see a bird flying about looking at a watch and needing to get to a board meeting on time. No, they function with the intuitive rhythm of life. All is well in their world without time. At one time humans lived this way too. The clock was invented only at the start of the fourteenth century. Realize that only the present is real. Learn from the past, and let it go. Revel in the wonderment of the timeless, eternal present, and live your life to the fullest!

The timeless in you is aware of life's timelessness, and knows that yesterday is but today's memory and tomorrow is today's dream.

–Khalil Gibran, Author–The Prophet

If you are dwelling in the past, you cannot help but suffer. You want something to be different from what it is now. This is how acceptance and presence go hand in hand. When you accept, you can live in presence. When you live in presence, you naturally accept. If you cannot accept what happened, you will never be able to live in presence. And by living in the now, you will naturally have no choice but to accept what is. You will experience the transformational power of acceptance and the many hidden gifts that true acceptance brings.

By staying in presence and acceptance, I have been able to respond to Sal's transition in a very different way than if my mind were wondering in dark, destructive thoughts of blame, guilt, and fear. Staying present allows me to be aware of all the signs that Sal sends me and to feel his essence with me at certain times. By being present I have not let my mind wander into scary, self-defeating thoughts of victimhood and loneliness. This is also described in detail in Part I, under acceptance.

When you live life from the present moment, you do not suffer. There are no real problems in this very moment. The storyteller, and the inner critic cannot survive in the present moment. They only live in the past and the future. The present moment is the only place where life is. The present moment is all there is—it is life. From the quote above by Eckhart Tolle, you can see that you, in your pure essence, are actually the present moment. You might even say that *you*, the *present moment*, and *life* are synonymous. At this moment, this may not make sense to you. But don't worry about that right now. All you have to do is hold presence, and you will soon know the truth by feeling it, not by thinking about it.

Presence Power

*The secret of health for both mind and body is not to mourn for the past,
not to worry about the future, and not to anticipate troubles, but to live the
present moment wisely and earnestly.*

–THE BUDDHA

How hard is it to stay in the present moment? It is actually quite difficult if you have lived your whole life avoiding it. The average person lives almost entirely identified with the thinker and is therefore living life in the past or the future. This is considered normal so it is not seen by most as a problem.

The truth is that when we live in the state of presence, life feels much better. When you live in presence, you dissolve time, or it could be said that presence causes time to stand still. Not clock time but psychological time, which is created by egoic thinking. Without time there is no suffering, no fear, and therefore, all negativity is dissolved.

When you are present you feel more relaxed. You actually hear the birds singing, you feel the warmth of the sun on your body, you smell the roses in the garden, and you see the beauty of nature in a new and fresh way. And best of all, you are not dwelling on your problems. So even though life feels better when we live in presence, we continuously fall back into "normal states of consciousness" which is living in the grip of the ego or living in a state where we are distracted from the joy of the present moment, because we are worrying about the future or feeling regret and sadness of something from the past.

Living in the present moment and moving through life in presence gives you a special power—the power to live life freely and fully without negativity, the power to relax and enjoy life, the power to live in acceptance and let go of fear and drama, and the power to feel and know that you are an infinite and eternal being. Presence allows you to know your true nature as the underlying invisible Infinite Intelligence that animates your body. Presence opens the door to realize this Infinite Intelligence is also in every creature, which then gives you the natural ability to *feel* the eternal Oneness of everything. This is what I call, Presence Power!

Awareness

Diligent Awareness is the first step to amp up presence power. To have a strong presence, which I will call presence power, and to stay in presence most of the time, awareness is the most important skill to develop. If you are enjoying presence and all of a sudden you notice that the storyteller or the inner critic moved in and is sweeping you away to the regrets of the past or the anxiety of the future, just notice and calmly come back to the present. You may do this by simply bringing your awareness to one deep, cleansing breath. All you need to do to come back to presence is to notice you have been swept away by the mind and take one slow consciousness breath. Also, congratulate yourself for noticing you dropped out of presence. If you noticed you got pulled into time, into incessant thoughts, your awareness was not gone for long. Without this awareness you might have just spent the rest of the day back to the "normal" state. In the East this is called, monkey mind. A mind jumping back and forth to past or future with each random thought that continuously comes into your mind. It almost feels like someone turned on a radio station in your head that you can't turn off! And the sad truth is that most humans are walking around with this random radio station on, thinking that these repetitive thoughts is who they are! This sounds insane and it is, but in our world it considered normal. By knowing the difference between presence and monkey mind you are on your way to leading a more peaceful existence..

It takes constant effort to be aware of your state of consciousness. You need to be a warrior of awareness to stay present. To hold presence gives you power for a more enjoyable and sacred life, a life of deep inner peace and joy.

Meditation Builds Presence Power

In Part IV, I go into detail on meditation. I only mention it here because it is an essential practice for building the habit of living in the present moment. Meditation is usually practiced sitting in silence. It can be done at any time and for any period of time, more commonly practiced in the mornings on average for twenty minutes. If you practice morning meditation, it typically leads you more effectively into a day of being present.

In summary meditation disciplines the mind and keeps us in the present moment. Meditation allows you to be aware and develop the witness consciousness, which makes it quite evident that you are not those incessant thoughts that you can't turn off. In meditation you may not be able to stop those thoughts, but you can shine the light of consciousness on the constant uninvited thoughts by simply observing them without judging them. This alone will slow down the thoughts, it's almost as if they know they are being watched. With practice you will eventually be able to stop or at least slow down those thoughts. At first it might only be for ten seconds but as you continue to practice meditation and presence, you will be able to go longer without any thought and you will enjoy the deep peace of being, also known as presence. This is presence power. Think of presence as living your life as a meditation.

Games Grow Presence Power

To develop a strong sense of presence power, I have to work out my presence muscles. Just like you have to work out your physical muscles daily in the gym for power and endurance; the same is true for developing presence power. When I was training for running half-marathons, I would train in the forest. I would tell myself, *just see if you could keep running until you get to that tree off in the distance.* If I made my goal small and attainable, I found I could keep running to the next tree and the next tree. Remember transformation does not happen in one big step but in many baby steps along the way.

So I took this same practice with developing my presence power. I went back to the forest, but this time I was just leisurely walking. I would challenge myself to walk to the tree off in the distance without a thought. Instead of thinking I would be totally immersed in sense perceptions. It was a shift from thinking and doing to just being and feeling. I would walk, feeling my feet making contact with the soft dirt ground; I would hear the stream and the birds, I would feel the breeze on my skin, and I would be aware of my breathing. However, I later found a way to further simplify this practice. For me it was using the sense of hearing. If I just put 100% of my awareness on listening to the sounds of the forest, my mind would be quiet. I would stop thinking as I moved more into just being. This being state allowed me to be totally present. It was getting easier and very comfortable living this way, at least in the forest and anywhere in nature. But I learned to take this practice with me wherever I went. I actually love to take it to San Francisco. To just walk around the city and hear the hum of cars, sirens, and people interacting. I could look in the shop windows at Union Square and enjoy all the beautiful things, without attachment, as I stayed in presence. It becomes very soothing even in busy, chaotic cities. I was tapping into the flow of life beyond the surface chaos.

Other games I play to amp up the presence power is to choose something I do repetitively throughout my day, such as walking up and down the steps in the house or at work. Every time I do steps, I make it a habit to become totally present. I get out of my head and feel the muscles in my body working to get me up or down the stairs. Sometimes I simply just concentrate on my breathing while climbing or descending the stairs.

If you have a job as I have had as a dental hygienist, which requires one to wash their hands twenty times a day, use that as your presence practice. I would immediately stop thinking about the past or present whenever I washed my hands, instead I would feel the soothing warm water on my hands and feel it running through my fingers. Water is amazing when you really look at it and feel it. I would smell the soap and feel the soap foaming up on my hands. I would feel the sensation of rubbing my hands together and getting them really soapy. This all happened in less than twenty seconds, and kept me in presence. I also use this same technique with washing the dishes at home, or any other repetitive tasks I do during the day.

For example, one can bring this same practice while getting in and out of the car. Before taking off, take a few deep, mindful breaths; do the same before hopping out of the car—pause a moment, relax and breathe, be present. If one practices this while eating one will find that you eat less and enjoy food more. Slow down while eating, smell the food before you eat it, chew it thoroughly instead of gulping it down. As one eats mindfully, excessive weight will naturally fall away and the enjoyment of food will increase.

If practicing at home, put a little post-it note on the stairs or by the sink to remind you to practice presence at these times. Because the first thing that will happen is that one will forget to do the presence practice, maybe because you were stressed and/or rushing around. The note will help remind you to do the practice and soon it will become a habit. Studies show that doing something for twenty-one days consecutively forms a habit, whether it is flossing your teeth or meditating. From consistently practicing presence while walking up and down the steps, washing your hands, or getting out of the car, the habit of being present will naturally flow into other areas of your life.

I do this practice with my students and it is fun to hear how everyone picked a different way to practice and how it helped to bring them to presence. Eventually this carries over to other areas of your life and the more presence you bring into your day, the better your day.

Feel the Inner Body

There is an aliveness that circulates throughout the body and even beyond the body. In the West we call this aliveness, *life force*, in India it is called *prana* and in China it is called *chi*. Vedic Sanskrit, one of the oldest languages on earth, translates *prana* into life force. Chi from ancient Chinese Taoism also translates to life force, or vital force, and is thought to be inherent in all things. To keep it simple, I will refer to this life force in the body and the *inner body*.

So what is this inner body? The inner body or life force is hard to describe in words and may be a different experience for different people. But as you read through this section, you will have a good idea of what it feels like, what it is, and what it can do. What the inner body feels like is a subtle tingling in the body, almost like when you feel the "chills." To feel the inner body is to have an awareness of the vibration within the body. To fully inhabit the body.

When you practice feeling the inner body, you will soon be able to feel it expand beyond the physical boundaries of the body. Remember that the inner body is energy that is formless so it can easily pass through the boundaries of the physical body. The inner body is not as dense as the physical body, but not as subtle as what we might call the formlessness. The inner body can be said to be a bridge from form to formlessness—a bridge from our physical body to our formless spirit.

When we feel the inner body, we come out of the mind, we stop our thinking, and we put our awareness on *feeling*, which then automatically anchors us in presence.

I sometimes see energy, and when I do, I see that we have a strong flow coming from our hands and feet. The first place to get familiar with feeling the inner body is to start feeling it in the palms of your hands. If you close your eyes and put all your awareness on your hands, can you feel that you have hands? When you put all your awareness on the hands you can feel them, from the inside out. This simply takes concentration and focus; most people can feel the life force in their hands if they try. Once you feel it in the hands, with continued concentration and practice, you then will feel it throughout the whole body.

Another way to make it easier to feel your inner body is to jump up and down and shake every part of your body or to run in place for about thirty seconds or longer and then stop and stand still and feel the tingling in the body. Or to tense every muscle of the body tightly for ten seconds or longer and then fully release all tension from the body. You can also do this one body part at a time if that is easier for you. I instruct my students to tighten all their muscles two to three times and then fully release all the tension—to be still and feel. This activates feeling the inner body and you will easily feel it throughout the whole body. The more you practice this, the easier it becomes and eventually you can feel it without any effort other than focusing on simply tuning in and feeling.

When you are able to feel the inner body throughout the whole body, you can run it as a wave of energy up and down the body, from the head to the toes. And then back up the body, from the toes to head. Do this several times up and down the body. I find that this practice keeps me healthy and amps up not only my presence power but also my immune system. And as an added bonus, it simply feels good. This is a very good practice to do as soon as you feel a cold coming on. Try it for yourself and see what happens. Feeling the inner body has also been found to be anti-aging. It is especially effective when done first thing in the morning before getting out of bed and last thing at night before you fall asleep. When you practice this as you fall asleep, it will promote a restful and peacefully deep sleep. Upon awakening in the morning, it will keep your state of mind focused and clear. With this practice you start and end your day in presence.

Feeling your inner body is a portal into the now and is a way to sense your nonphysical loved one. It is a doorway to connect with the spirit world. As well as anchoring yourself in stillness where you need to be, to feel your formless loved ones and your own essence. Eventually we come to know that connecting with our departed loved ones is our bridge to our own true essence and to Source.

Nature and Presence

Nature provides an environment that is very conducive to being in the present moment. I have already mentioned this in the section above, titled *Games Grow Presence Power*. Nature is also covered in chapter nine. One of the reasons for this is that nature is mostly still and calm, but not always. For example, the trees in the forest are still. One can say that the stillness of the trees in the forest encourages us to be still and quiet in our minds, so our thoughts quiet down.

When we are in a place of solitude, such as a forest, a mountain top, the sea or dessert, there is a beautiful silence, except for the occasional sound of the wind, a stream, the pounding of the waves on the sand, a birdsong, or another subtle nature sound. We can easily become quiet, and enjoy being held in the silence of our environment, especially if we are by ourselves. When we are in an environment that is deeply quiet, it allows us to be still and quiet within, to be present. But to be still within does not always mean we need to be still without. We can walk and function in life with a still and present mind.

Nature doesn't have to be quiet and still to promote presence in us. When Mother Nature blows her wind through the trees of the forest, it creates a symphony of rustling leaves and a light show of dancing shadows—this can bring contentment. Even the sound of rain can bring us a sense of calmness and ease. Why, because nature is already present. Nature does not know how to be anything, but present. Animals are the same way, which is why our pets can be great teachers for us of presence and unconditional love.

Presence and future

Everything is energy and that's all there is to it. Match the frequency of the reality you want and you cannot help but get that reality. It can be no other way. This is not philosophy, this is physics.

–ALBERT EINSTEIN, PHYSICIST

The greatest determinant of our future is our state of consciousness at this moment. This makes us realize that our state of consciousness is also our greatest responsibility. We don't have to worry about how our state of consciousness was in the past or how it will be in the future—no just focus on how is it right now. When you look deeply, you begin to realize that how you are feeling is directly related to the thoughts you are thinking. When you stop to feel your emotions, you realize they are directly related to your thoughts. You then realize that your future is being shaped by the state of your consciousness at this moment. If you are feeling grateful and content, you are attracting abundance. If you are filled with intense anger, you are attracting irritating circumstances.

Therefore, the best practice for a positive future is to stay aware of your thoughts and feelings. Are you enjoying this moment or are you rushing to be in another moment? Is your mind running you? Or are you the master of your mind? The more presence power you have, the more awareness you have. The most important skill to learn for mastering your life here on earth is being aware. Without awareness of your thoughts, feelings, and emotions you have no clue what is going on and you are just bobbing on the surface of life. This is when people feel they are victims of life. Life is just happening to them and they feel completely helpless. However, we are actually powerful, creative beings.

With awareness you can stay in a positive state of mind or at the least be in acceptance of what is at that moment. And the more present and relaxed you are in this moment, the more open you are to allowing life to flow through you without tension, resistance, or drama.

We are creative beings and whether we know it or not we are constantly creating. Our perception of reality creates our thoughts and our thoughts create what happens next. We and everything else in the universe are energy, as physicists have proven for quite some time now. Quantum physics clearly reveals that we are all vibrating clusters of energy, as supported by Einstein's quote at the beginning of this section. However, we are all vibrating differently. A well-established law of physics is that like attracts like and so our energy is constantly attracting to us a perfect match. Just like the saying goes, *I got up on the wrong side of the bed today, and now everything is going wrong.* It means I woke up and immediately focused on my problems; I was in regret of the past and anxiety of the future. Now I feel grumpy and everybody is annoying me. Everything that could go wrong is going wrong.

The same is true when you get up on the right side of the bed and everything is flowing beautifully. This means *I woke up in a state of nonresistance; I am feeling love and gratitude just to be alive today.* This person did not immediately go straight to their problems or make a list for the day of all the endless chores they need to get done. This person is aware and stops their mind as it drifts to anxious or worrisome thoughts. They give full attention to what is at hand in the moment, even if it is as simple as walking down the stairs or across the room.

Ever notice how this happens? When you get up on the "right side of the bed," and stay present, you stay in a positive state of mind. Or when you get up on the "wrong side of the bed," and go into the past, worn-out, repetitive thought patterns of "my problems," you live in a negative state of mind. If you haven't noticed this, begin to pay attention and test it out for yourself. The tables can turn one way or the other, so stay alert and aware to your thoughts and what is going on in your mind. Life is always responding to our thoughts, which are a form of vibration. We simply need to pay attention to what is happening inside. Sometimes we cannot change our circumstances, but we do always have a choice of how we react to them. We always have a choice to be present and to think the thoughts that serve us. Are we coming from a place of love or fear?

With practice you can become more aware of your thoughts and emotions. A good way to practice getting back to presence, if you find yourself swept away by thoughts of the past or future, is to simply take one conscious breath. Relax and do not judge yourself. Use the power of breath to anchor yourself in the present. The breath works magic as has been previously discussed in the book. It is the best antidote with no side effects and it's free! Become aware of the breath and let it ground you in presence. The sooner you catch it, the easier it is to become present again.

Sometimes our minds can be like a wild animal, completely out of control. Sometimes the only thing we can do is simply observe the crazy, destructive thoughts. Accept that right now we can't change our mood and choose to ignore any negative thoughts and negative emotions. We do not have to believe every thought that comes to us. We do not need to identify with any of these random, repetitive thoughts. We can be aware of what we are feeling and we can just accept that we are not feeling great right now. We can feel comfort in knowing that this bad mood will soon pass and this mood is in no way us! All we need to do is simply stay in the seat of the observer and of acceptance. We can do what we can to distract ourselves. Take a nap if you can or call a friend, watch comedy on YouTube, play a video game, or go to a movie. Or just take one conscious breath at a time and say to yourself, *This will pass; I am not these thoughts or this feeling.* Just observe the bad mood if you can't release it and it will soon dissipate, because it will not get charged like it does when you identify with it. You keep it at a distance by just observing it as a stranger inhabiting your psyche for a while. But you are still in charge; you are on to this bad mood, which is coming from past pain. It is usually past pain that comes up to strengthen itself. You weaken it overtime, as you step back and simply observe it without identifying with it. Thereby, not allowing it to enter your pristine inner world and take you over. By diligently practicing this, it will eventually disappear for good.

We are human and mastering our emotions and thoughts and building presence power is a process for most people. It rarely happens overnight. And it is not easy; most of us were not raised with these skills. Most of us were taught our life skills in school and home, and they were to focus on developing reason and logic. We did not learn life skills such as meditation, acceptance, presence and forgiveness, to deal effectively with life's challenges. These skills are not taught to children in school, even though these important skills contribute to a successful life, a life of peace and happiness.

Acceptance

Learn to get in touch with the silence within yourself and know that everything in this life has a purpose.

–Elisabeth Kübler-Ross, Psychiatrist, Author

The Five Stages of Grief. Really?

The Kübler-Ross model

1. Denial

2.Anger

3. Depression

4. Bargaining

5. Acceptance

When I was a senior in college, I had an assignment to read Elisabeth Kübler-Ross's book, *On Death and Dying.* This book had a profound impact on my life that has never left me. I later read many of her other books. What I took away from her profound teachings in her book, was that when you are on your death bed you do not regret that you took a risk and took your two young sons to Europe by yourself for two months on a shoe-string budget or that you followed your heart and did the work you loved knowing the money would follow. What you might regret is that you were so responsible and such a good girl that you put yourself behind everyone else and did not follow your dreams. Instead you listened to logic and not your heart and you spent all your time pleasing others. That is what I took from her book. I am in gratitude to her for these great insights that she was teaching in the seventies; she was a woman ahead of her time.

From her book, I also learned the five stages patients go through when diagnosed with a terminal disease. They are those listed above. These later became known as the five stages of grief as well. I would like to note that in either case these are not recommended stages but rather they are *observed* stages that people in her study went through when they were given a death sentence, from a terminal illness diagnosis.

From her quote above, it is evident that she did not intend for people to expect to go through all these stages, it is an *observation* of what the average person did. These five stages are what Elisabeth Kübler-Ross observed from people who were in the dying process, not from those grieving from a loss of a loved one. These stages are not mandatory to reach acceptance. If you did not go into denial or depression, but went into anger and then acceptance, that is ok. And it is possible to go into shock and then straight into acceptance. But it is important to remember that everyone grieves in his or her own way. Denial can be absolutely necessary; for many, denial is a very important mechanism for survival. Most children go into denial when traumatized because they do not have the skills to do anything else and their very survival depends on denial.

One of the reasons many do not go into acceptance first is that they actually do not know this is even possible. They may feel that they need to go through, denial, anger, and depression. Many feel this sequence is what is expected of us when we lose a loved one. And that if we do not go through these five stages, we might be missing something. Some may even feel guilty if they appear to have an inner peace after the tragic loss. And may feel they have to uphold a self-image of a grieving person.

This expectation of going into denial and then becoming angry and depressed is an old paradigm of the grieving process and will eventually dissolve as we evolve. This is significant for three reasons: one is because it is simply unhealthy and unnecessary to continue to live in despair. We will inevitably get physically sick, as many studies have shown. We were meant to be joyful and loving beings. Being authentically happy, cheerful, and positive are qualities of the soul. Two, we would never awaken or have any growth if we did not transcend and learn from our traumatic experiences in life. Acceptance is a major teacher and healer, and if you get stuck in depression or anger, you may never get to the invaluable transformation acceptance offers.

Bliss arises from the soul. This unconditional joy is not emotion.

–ELLEN GRACE O'BRIAN, AUTHOR

The **third** important reason for a shift in the traditional grief paradigm is that our passed loved ones would never want us to live a life of despair because of them. Also, we would be absent for our loved ones here on earth who love us and want us to be part of their lives

Please do not get me wrong, it is normal and healthy to be broken-hearted and feel pain from the loss of a loved one. Everyone needs to get to acceptance on their own terms and in their own way, without judgment from themselves or anyone else. And no one should ever feel bad about traveling the journey of loss and grief in their own time frame. It is important to reach acceptance eventually. And it takes time to heal from a deep loss, even if you are in acceptance immediately.

One greatly benefits by being aware that you do not have to go through all five stages unless you feel you need to. My point is—you are no longer expected to go through all the five stages. And most importantly you do not have to suffer in depression for the rest of your life; there is another way. Once you dwell in denial, anger, and depression, it is clear you are dwelling in the past. It can then become a way of life for you; the brain adjusts to living in the past. The longer you do this, the harder it is to get back to a life of peace, joy, and love. I know this from direct experience by observing my own mother and other clients who have lost children.

In reality, a loss of any kind that is perceived as insurmountable can drive one to a life of despair. This is why practicing presence is so important, it pulls you out of living in the past. Living a life of presence will lead you directly to acceptance and peace. What sometimes brings many people to acceptance, is that they just get tired of feeling bad. For others feeling bad can feel safe and comfortable. It can then become your identity and sadly it is rare that these people recover. This reality is heartbreaking. Dwelling on negative emotions produces a downward spiral; it has a hypnotic rhythm that can take you down to a bottomless pit. This is also true for the positive side as well. If you dwell on presence and acceptance, that same hypnotic rhythm will take your life to higher levels of intrinsic peace and happiness.

There is a difference between feeling the pain of heartbreak and prolonged suffering. Prolonged suffering can last a lifetime and we can become self-absorbed and lose ourselves in constant suffering. The wise person uses suffering for transcendence, and acceptance is the key to transcend suffering.

Acceptance Leads to Transformation

Hope is the golden cord connecting you to heaven.

–SARAH YOUNG, AUTHOR

Finding *meaning* and experiencing *spiritual transcendence* can be viewed as a *sixth step* of grief, in the evolution of human beings. Acceptance can lead to spiritual growth, meaning an open heart full of compassion, a deep inner peace, and so forth; this has already been spoken of in Part I. Acceptance to loss of any kind can also lead to seeing meaning in the loss. For example, I was able to communicate with Sal only two days later because I was in acceptance. When I did connect I was told of our sacred contract and then later I actually remembered agreeing to our sacred contract in a lucid dream. This sacred contract gave meaning to Sal's early departure. Another example is, I was able to lose my fear of death because I understood from direct experience that death is the opposite of birth, not the opposite of life and that love/life knows no death, and so on; these insights and many more are shared throughout this book. Sal's death lead me in a strong way to fully realized there is no death and our consciousness, which is the true Self, continues. This gave even more meaning to Sal's life and death. The fact that many of his young friends realized this truth of the continuation of life, gave meaning to Sal's transition.

I have worked one on one with many cancer patients who are now healed, many have told me that their cancer was a gift. The cancer caused them to lead their life in a totally different way, a better way. They no longer hold on to anger; they have a healthier lifestyle, they are eating well, exercising, and meditating. They accepted their illness that led them to find meaning in the tragedy of their situation. If someone close to you had cancer and did not survive, it could mean that on a soul level they were ready to make their transition. Every case is individual and completely different. And whether they survived or not does not qualify whether they found meaning or not from their illness. The ones who found meaning tend to be the ones who transformed. There are many people who have huge spiritual transformations before they make their transition; this is a beautiful occurrence and leads to a peaceful transition.

The Practice of Acceptance

Acceptance doesn't mean resignation; it means understanding that something is what it is and that there's got to be a way through it.

– MICHAEL J. FOX

I had first learned acceptance from all the spiritual books I had been reading over the years. My meditation classes organically evolved into teaching classes on surrender and acceptance. I had been practicing surrender in my own life on little things, then on bigger things, and finally on everything. I was not always successful right away, but what I found is that if you stick with the practice, it becomes more and more natural.

I write about how I went into acceptance the night we lost Sal, in Part I. So here I will focus more on how you can put acceptance into practice in your everyday life, if you choose to. I will use the words surrender and acceptance interchangeably.

Many people have a hard time with the word surrender. Because they think of the white flag held up in war from the side that is surrendering, the side that lost and is giving up, and may become prisoners. But quite the opposite is meant here by surrender; it is empowering and intelligent. Surrendering is not giving up; it is *stepping up* to living a life of wonderment. You are not surrendering to the "bad guys," you are surrendering to the intelligent life force behind the universe. Some say it this way; Let go and let God. If the word surrender, doesn't work for you, just substitute this word with acceptance, allow, or let life flow.

The act of surrender is simple yet the results are profound. The act of surrendering is allowing life to flow, saying yes to life rather than resisting what is. The only place you can experience the flow of life is in the present moment. You cannot feel the flow of life in the past or in the future. So to surrender is to accept the present moment as it is, without hesitation or resistance. When you become present you naturally live a life of surrender.

When things go wrong is when we most often go into resistance. We go into resistance by the mind judging and making up stories about whatever it is that we feel has gone wrong. When things go wrong is the most important time to accept what is, in order to prevent pain and suffering in your life. Resistance happens when we are only identified with the thinker. When we live a life of surrender we naturally begin to live life in alignment with Source, with God.

Although acceptance is the first step and the most important step in a difficult situation, it helps to remember that it should be practiced in everyday life as a way of living your life, not just something you pull out when something traumatic happens. Try practicing acceptance first on the little things and it will naturally flow to the bigger things in life. You will begin to see the positive affects the practice of acceptance has on your life and it will eventually become the way you operate in the world. If you are already practicing it on the small things, when something traumatic comes up in your life, you will be in practice and it will be easier for you.

Here are some examples of practicing acceptance on the little things in life. Resistance and negativity work hand in hand. We may be practicing resistance in little ways that we do not even realize. If you are complaining about the weather, you are in resistance. We do not have any control over the weather, so why complain about it and wish it was different? Is complaining about it going to change it? No it's not, so why waste your time and energy? It makes no sense. Most of this behavior is learned behavior. However, that is not a good enough reason to continue to complain about things that cannot be changed. The truth is, when we complain about anything, we are practicing resistance. So accept the weather for what it is; this is a first step to living a life of acceptance. Don't judge yourself if you find yourself complaining about little things. I think most of us witnessed this in our parents, teachers, and other influential people in our lives. And it is mostly just a bad habit. But once you see it for what it really is, a practice of resistance, you will be motivated to let it go. When you let it go, you will feel better. Try it out for yourself.

Many nice people get in their cars and turn into angry drivers when given the opportunity. Do you or anyone you know experience that kind of aggression called, *road rage*? This is practicing resistance and negativity. Does the neighbors' barking dog send you into a frenzy? These are all wonderful opportunities to practice acceptance and presence. Think of these triggers as great teachers, great opportunities to point out that you have a choice to practice either resistance and negativity or acceptance.

You can think of resistance as a NO to life and surrender as a YES to life. When you say no to life by being in resistance, you are fighting with life and life can then become difficult. You may not even realize this connection.

When you think about it, our life and our world is really an outer reflection of the inner world of our thoughts and perceptions. Are we totally identified with our minds and bodies as who we are? If we are doing this, then we are living only from our egos or lower self? Or are we aware of our true essence, our inner being? You can think of a mirror, as a metaphor, to demonstrate how our inner and outer worlds are connected. When you resist life, it is like fighting with your reflection in the mirror. We understand that the image in the mirror, reflects back to you. When you smile at the mirror you know for sure the image in the mirror is going to smile right back at you. As the image in the mirror reflects back to you, your outer world reflects back to your inner world, your thoughts, attitudes, and perceptions. Is the way you live inside full of resistance or acceptance? This is what is reflecting back to you.

When one lives a life of resisting what is, not living in the present, not going with the flow of life, but rather living in the past in regret or in the future filled with angst and anxiety, life can feel very unfriendly on the outside. But when one stays in the flow of life by being present, feeling inner peace, and has a deep inner knowing and faith that all is well, life appears much more friendly. When you trust in the divine order of the universe, when you are friends with life, life seems to flow for you. You may experience constant synchronicities, divine timing, and feel you are lucky. Things somehow always seem to work out for you, people are nice to you for the most part. I think we all know the feeling of *being in the flow*.

This is not to say that challenges will not arise for one who lives in presence and surrender; challenges will continue to come up. But because you will respond intelligently to these challenges, the drama will diminish considerably.

Another practical example of how life has no choice but to fight back when you are in negativity and resistance would be to go back to the topic of road rage. You always have a choice if someone cuts you off to just let it go, no drama. Or you could get very angry and flip the guy off while screaming obscenities. This will be sure to increase your heart rate, blood pressure, and cortisol levels (stress hormones). All this is bad for your health, and now something even worse may happen. By screaming at the driver who cut you off, you have now dropped down to a lower vibration and are engaging in antagonizing him. He may slam on his brakes so you will rear-end him. And now you have to deal with insurance and a lot of unnecessary drama.

Life just got harder because you chose resistance. But let's look at this situation from a place of simple common sense. How hard was it for you to just let this go? It really is very simple and empowering to let this go. But it takes a certain amount of conscious awareness to stop the old habitual knee-jerk reaction and move to responding intelligently by not letting it bother you. How do we do that?

Resistance

Whatever you resist you become. If you resist sadness,
you are always sad. If you resist suffering, you are always suffering.
We think that we resist certain states because they are there, but actually
they are there because we resist them.

-ADYASHANTI, AUTHOR

To stop doing this, you have to be diligent in observing your thoughts, your speech, and actions. You have to be alert enough to catch this behavior so you can stop wasting time and energy and so you can move into a life filled with ease and peace. Start by recognizing there is resistance. You can recognize resistance by noticing you are thinking negative thoughts. You can also notice the physical sensations resistance brings to the body. Such as a tensing of muscles, tightening of neck and shoulders, clenching of the jaw, grinding the teeth, increase in heart rate, shallowness of breathing. Just recognizing one of these symptoms of resistance is enough.

The earlier you can detect yourself falling into the trap of knee-jerk reactions, the better. Because the sooner you catch the ego at it antics, the easier it is to stop it. If you are not alert, before you know it, you may find yourself screaming back at the unconscious driver who cut you off. The ego is going to want to defend itself. The wiser part of you, your inner being, will not be bothered and will easily let it go. The ego will tell you that you are being weak if you just let it go. But the opposite is true of course; the intelligence of your inner being is going to have no problem letting it go and knows that the power is in surrender. Through the power of surrender there is now no drama, no stress; you just remain in peace and presence as you continue your drive. When you get really good at this, you may even bless the unaware person who cut you off. We never know what other people are going through and it is not our place to judge others, it depletes our energy. At first you may feel vulnerable when you practice surrender but remember empowerment, not weakness, comes from vunerability.

Vulnerability is not winning or losing; it's having the courage to show up and be seen when we have no control over the outcome.

–BRENE BROWN, PHD, AUTHOR

The reason it is so easy for your inner being to let it go, is that your inner being is not identified with the body and thoughts (that part of you is the ego) so there is nothing to defend. If someone insults you and you are more identified with your inner being than the ego, it will just pass though you, as there is no resistance to block it. You know your consciousness, cannot be threaten. When you come from this place, there is no effort in surrender, it is more natural for you. For a person like this, it would feel completely uncomfortable to react in a defensive manner, and that kind of reaction would take much more effort for them.

With practice you will be able to move to the witness consciousness and witness the resistance in yourself. The more you practice this, the easier it will be to stay in that place of observation when the ego uses it's antics to get you to go into resistance. You can imagine the ego as a toddler who just doesn't know any better. And who wants your attention. You will get to the point where you can just be aware of these feelings to defend, react, and resist and know that these pulls are not You. They are the ego, the false small self that thrives on drama. Hold to that place of the observer, the witness, and let the light of your conscious awareness dissolve the urge to defend and to react. You will then know how to respond or if you actually need to respond. If you want to be the master of your life, stay with the quieter voice of the Infinite Intelligence within you.

Many feel that if you surrender to what is, you cannot change it. When something goes wrong and you accept it, it allows the situation to change with ease, rather than with effort and force. Surrendering can transform a situation that can be changed. You may need to take action to change it or it may just happen on its own.

I have come to learn that when you go into acceptance on something you *cannot* change, the situation will not change but *you will change*. When you accept, you will actually use the situation for transcendence, for awakening. Living a life of surrender always transforms us and if possible, our life situation. It brings us home to our true Selves.

Anyone could choose to live a life of surrender. You don't need a difficult challenge, either. You just need the desire to live from a higher place. Living a life of surrender and presence can lead to awakening and to a life of peace and harmony.

CHAPTER NINE:

Morning Practice

**Meditation ~ Prayer ~ Affirmation-Mantra ~ Intention ~
Yoga Movement ~ Breathing ~ Health ~ Energy Medicine ~
Emotional Freedom Technique ~ Journaling ~ Nature**

If you look at the lives of the most successful individuals, from champion athletes, to influential leaders, to enlightened masters, they all lead a life of self-discipline. The awakened ones have consistent practices of meditation, as the athlete practices his sport consistently for hours each day. To live a successful life, a life filled with love and peace, we need to have enough self-discipline to commit to a daily practice and lifestyle changes that promote a positive emotional state, a strong mind, a healthy body, and a deep spiritual connection. We also need a continuous commitment to be alert to our thoughts, to stay in presence. This takes self-discipline and constant awareness. And is the most crucial discipline for awakening. This was already discussed in the *Presence* section.

The practices and lifestyle changes in this section are mainly what I have been studying, teaching, and practicing for over thirty-five years. These practices have helped my students, myself and others to heal from life challenges and to live a healthy and balanced life. Sure in the process there will be resistance to deal with, but trusting in the process, doing the work, and taking one day at time, sometimes even one breath at a time, is what leads to healing and thriving. Our mindset is imperative to the way our lives play out. Chapter Ten will cover the importance of the mindset.

Life on earth is not easy, but staying centered and dedicated to a morning practice and healthy lifestyle has the ability to keep us balanced and grounded when life gets shaky. With these abilities we can experience life's adversaries as a path to allow for posttraumatic *growth*, rather than posttraumatic *stress disorder*. And most importantly a life of awakening to our true Selves, a life of being "awake in this cosmic dream" as Yogananda describes it. Or as Jesus puts it, having the awareness to "be in this world, but not of this world."

It may look like there are a lot of activities listed here as a morning practice, but many of them are used together. I like to start the day with meditation, which starts with a prayer; many in fact consider meditation as a silent prayer. The mantra, affirmations, and intention are all part of meditation. I may end my meditation with a few minutes of EFT (emotional freedom technique) and some journaling. I like to do some yoga after meditation, but this can be any kind of movement you prefer. Yoga is a form of energy medicine and I may add in the five-minute routine by Donna Eden or energizations exercises as mention under the energy medicine section. Working with breathing is used throughout the day with a special focus on breathing techniques during meditation and yoga. I try to get out into nature every day, not only for cardio exercises, but also to soak up the beauty of nature, which has been scientifically shown to reduce stress and increase mental clarity. Eating healthy and exercising becomes a lifestyle and takes no effort after you have make it a permanent way of being in the world. So just like brushing our teeth every morning becomes a habit, we can add in a morning or afternoon practice of what brings us joy, peace, and health. Why wouldn't we do this?

Meditation

*Even a little practice of meditation will free you from dire fears
and colossal sufferings*

−BHAGAVAD GITA

Meditation and mindfulness/presence are interwoven throughout this book; however, this section is dedicated to the daily practice of meditation. I attribute meditation and presence practice as the reason I am able to positively deal with Sal's death and many other challenges in my life, rather than succumbing to depression and loss of enthusiasm for life. In yoga, the Sanskrit term used for spiritual practice is called *sadhana*. My morning practice of meditation is my *sadhana* and it's the most important part of my day to help me maneuver through life's challenges and through times of uncertainty. Your *sadhana* is your rock-solid anchor; do it every day.

Life can be scary at times and we need to build a solid foundation to deal with times of uncertainty and adversity. Meditation is that solid foundation that helps to keep us anchored in faith and a deep inner peace. Silence is said to be the language of God. It is in silence, which we experience in meditation, that we begin to uncover our anchor of knowing we are eternal beings and nothing can threaten us. At our deepest core we know we are infinite spiritual beings and life continues indefinitely for us. We realize that this earth life is but a blink of an eye in eternity.

It is said that prayer is talking to God, while meditation is listening to God. In meditation we train our mind to quiet down, to stop the chatter in the head, so that we can be open to receive that which is beyond the thinking mind, so that we can reach Infinite Intelligence. When the thinker is quiet, we can actually hear, feel, and tune into the wise Consciousness behind the incessant thoughts.

Many ancient cultures describe life as dream or an illusion. The science of quantum physics also demonstrates scientifically that everything in life is energy, and reality as we know it is not as real and solid as it appears to be. When we look at our hand, a table or even a rock, it appears to be solid, but quantum physics says we are 99.9% space. We are a bundle of vibrating molecules. I have already spoken of this.

Quantum physicists are quite clearly showing that everything is energy at the most fundamental levels. Early in the 20th century the unquestioned assumption that the physical universe is actually physical lead to a scientific search for the elementary "point particle" upon which all life is built, which would prove that reality was not an illusion. But as soon as scientists began smashing electrons and other particles in enormous accelerators, they quickly realized the foundations of the physical world weren't physical at all—that everything is energy.

The Scientific Proof That Everything is Energy and Reality Isn't Real

–Cate Montana, MA, Author

In ancient Hindu philosophy, life on earth is called *maya*, Sanskrit for illusion. *A Course in Miracles* teaches that life on earth is a dream. Almost all the great spiritual teachers from every corner of earth and every walk of life agree—life on earth has a dreamlike quality to it. Many modern-day scientists would agree. Even Albert Einstein, who was born in 1879, said, "Reality is merely an illusion, although a very persistent one." Could it be that the formless realm is reality? And if life is like a dream, what are we dreaming and why are we dreaming at all? Can it be that the universe is becoming conscious of itself through us? Can it be we are dreaming that we are nothing more than this body and these thoughts we have in our heads? When we think of ourselves as only bodies and thoughts, we are in our ego, our small self. When we awaken, we realize that we are much more than just a body and a mind that has repetitive thoughts. When we awaken we realize that we have been dreaming that we are these little helpless human beings, but in actuality, our true Self has no fear because it knows its formless reality and it knows it is not separate from the whole.

I know in my own experience I really didn't get into meditation until I had a meditation teacher. I feel the best way to really learn meditation and establish a practice is to have a meditation teacher that you resonate with. In this book, I will not attempt to teach meditation but will simply explain how it works and then you can decide if you want to take it further.

It is never too late to learn to meditate. And you do not need to meditate for long before you feel the benefits of meditation. Even ten to twenty minutes in the morning can make a significant difference in your life. The key is to keep meditation consistent in your life, like brushing your teeth. So if you only have five minutes, do it! Tomorrow you can do it for longer, just keep it as consistent as you can, and if for some reason you fall out of the habit, do not criticize or judge yourself, just pick it up and begin again. You may find that you want to meditate more once you start the practice and notice the benefits. You will come to love your meditation time. But don't make it a chore, or a to-do list item, see it as a gift you are giving yourself to relax and honor yourself for doing something good for your well-being. There is nothing more beneficial than meditating, for your body, mind, and soul.

There are many different ways to meditate. Most of the time when people talk about meditation, they are referring to sitting meditation. Besides sitting meditation there is the practice of sleep-based meditation called *yoga nidra*, for which, you need to lie down. Lying down allows you to relax and go into the alpha, theta, and even delta brain waves while staying conscious. Apart from these, you have the walking meditation, the standing meditation, and the dancing meditation, and forest bathing and many more ways of meditation. For this discussion, I will be addressing sitting meditation.

Meditation is the practice of paying full attention on the present moment, by focusing your awareness on a mantra, your breathing, inner body, sense perceptions, or even a mandala or a candle. The breath is a very important part of meditation. Different practices will give you different ways to breathe. Keeping closed eyes gently lifted upward at the brow center shifts the consciousness to a higher state and prevents one from falling asleep.

A mantra is a simple prayer or affirmation that you repeat upon the inhalation and the exhalation. For example, you can use the mantra *So Hum*. As you breath in, you mentally say *So*, and as you breathe our, you mentally say *Hum*. You continue to repeat this mantra as you breathe. A mantra can be in Sanskrit or in English. *So Hum* is a Sanskrit mantra; in English, it translates to: I am that or I am spirit. You can also say these mantras in your native language if that is more comfortable for you. However, the Sanskrit mantra's can hold a high vibration, as evidenced by its use in meditation for more than three thousand years in the East. You can also just simply focus on the breath or sense perceptions or on feeling the aliveness in your body.

Meditation and presence are the best practices to shift the old paradigm of believing you are your incessant thoughts to coming to the realization that you are the spacious awareness behind the thoughts. Meditation demonstrates that there is the witnessing presence, which you could call your true essence or inner being, and there is the voice in the mind, which you can call the ego. In the practice of both presence and meditation, you are present and you are aware of thoughts, without judging them.

There is nothing more important to true growth than realizing that you are not the voice of the mind - you are the one who hears it.

–MICHAEL A. SINGER, AUTHOR–THE UNTETHERED SOUL

When you first learn to meditate, you will soon notice that there are two of you inside—the one observing the thoughts and the one thinking the thoughts. As you begin to look a little deeper, you will come to realize that the one thinking the thoughts, the voice of the mind, is not really you. Why? Because you will notice that the thoughts surface without any doing on your part. You will also notice that it is very difficult to turn off the thoughts; they are mostly random and repetitive. The National Science Foundation says we have an average of sixty thousand thoughts in a day; sadly 95% are repetitive, while 80% are negative. It is like having a radio on in your head that you can't seem to turn off. It is at this point you will realize you are the witness consciousness, the observer behind the thoughts, the spacious awareness, and the silent stillness that has always been there for as long as you could remember. The voice of the mind is loud; the witness is quiet but you can feel it and sometimes hear it, if you are still. Meditation is the practice of sitting in stillness.

As you become present in meditation, you will feel and maybe hear an intuitive voice coming from the deep stillness within, from a dimension beyond thinking that is more intelligent. When you think from this place, your thinking is clear and insightful.

It is important to realize that when you first begin to meditate, many negative memories and thoughts may arise. Do not worry about this or stop meditating because of this. We tend to suppress difficult times in our lives so we can cope. Children are very good at this; it is essential for their survival to do so. It is good that these repressed memories, both recent and from childhood, are surfacing. Allow them to rise and release them without a strong reaction or resistance. Observe them without judgment and let old, worn-out memories pass right through you. This is a beautiful cleansing; your fear of them has held them down. When you see how easy it is to let them go without judgment or comment, you will be happy they came up. Eventually this phase will pass and you will experience a deep peace that comes with continued meditation practice.

Sitting meditation is not for everyone. For you, meditation might be a walk in nature, gardening, painting, yoga nidra, guided meditation, or something else that holds you in presence. The most important thing to remember here is to do what works best for you. What brings you peace of mind? What quiets the inner critic and keeps you focused, alert, passionate, and present? Whatever that is for you, make it your consistent morning practice. Why morning? It doesn't have to be morning, but I find it is best in the morning because you are starting your day with positivity and calmness. I find it is most effective to go into meditation as soon as I wake, because my mind is already quiet and is more accessible to receiving the Infinite Intelligence. Make sure to do your practice before looking at your phone or emails, meditate when the mind is fresh and open to all the benefits that meditation has to offer.

Through meditation and stillness, we realize that when our bodies die, there is a part of us that does not die. The part of us that has always been there and will always Be. It is constant. It feels like unconditional love, peace, clarity, and truth. This awakening occurs little by little in our practice of presence and meditation and leads to awakening. For most of us awakening to our true Selves is a process. As we become aware of what we are not, the essence of who we truly are comes to the foreground.

If you read the studies on meditation you will learn the many healing benefits of meditation. Google the studies on the positive benefits of meditation, and they seem to be endless. Some of the benefits of meditation that have been found by scientific studies are improved mental clarity, decreased cellular inflammation, lowered blood pressure, lowered cortisol levels, healthy heart rate, and decreased depression. Meditation increases happiness, creativity, kindness, compassion, sense of humor, and immunity. These are just a few of the many positive benefits of a daily meditation practice.

The body, mind, and soul all benefit from meditation practice. However, the main purpose of meditation is to attain enlightenment. But on your way to enlightenment, you will sleep better at night, improve your memory, and decrease your stress, pain, cholesterol, and anxiety. I call all these benefits the positive side effects of meditation.

Some closing thoughts and definitions of meditation:

...when the mind and body are still and the heart is open

...remembering who and what you really are: a divine spirit, ever perfect, ever free (feeling a connection with all that is)

...a discipline; it takes practice and a willingness to form new habits. To develop an alert stillness, recognizing when you drift into random thoughts, takes willpower

... concentration; learning to focus on one thing at a time, it strengthens the mind.

...meant to change every aspect of your life; the test of your success in meditation is not in visions or what you hear, or feel in meditation, but rather how you are changing as a person in everyday life; the goal is to have your whole life become meditation

Prayer

Prayer is talking to God; Meditation is listening to God.

—St. Francis of Assisi

The most important thing to know about prayer, is to pray as though what you are praying for is already true for you. To feel in your entire being what it would feel like if it were already manifested. I also like to add in all my prayers that whatever it is I am praying for is for the highest good for all. If your prayers have an altruistic intention, I believe that when they do manifest, they will bring a fulfillment that does not come with selfish material requests. Nothing is wrong with praying from your materialistic self or your ego, but those items usually do not bring lasting happiness. And praying from ego is just not as effective. The new car or big house are nice but after a while that happiness fades. As compared to praying for peace in the family or the community. With peace comes lasting happiness.

It is also important to *not* pray as a *beggar*; you are made in the image and likeness of God. You can even say, you are a droplet of God. If you have had the experience of contacting the Oneness within, through meditation, you will know this to be true. If your Source/God were the ocean, you are a wave. If your Source was the sun, you are a ray of sunshine. It is important to realize that you and everyone and everything is a droplet of the One Source. When you truly feel this, you live on a whole different plane of reality. Knowing that when you harm the earth, an animal, or another human being, you are also harming your own essence. Realize your prayers will be heard if spoken with deep conviction, intention, and sincerity as a calm, loving demand. Know that your silent words have been heard and will be answered at the right time and in the best manner for all involved.

Children Intuitively Know How to Pray

You may say I'm a dreamer, but I'm not the only one,
I hope someday you'll join us, and the world will live as one.

–JOHN LENNON, MUSICIAN, SONG WRITER

When I was in third grade, I prayed every night to God that our family would be graced with a baby. At nine years old, I did not realize that my mom and dad might not want for this to happen. My mom was in her early forties and already had five kids; she was done with having kids. But I did not go to my mom and ask for a new baby in the family, I went straight to Source. I played this happy game every night using my imagination. Each night as I fell asleep, I would imagine that I was playing with the most adorable baby. I would have so much fun playing with this baby. I would take this baby everywhere with me, and teach it everything I knew. I felt all the love I would have for this baby and I felt all the joy and love it would bring to the family and to me. I did not put a sex on the baby; I left that up to God. I played this game in the present tense every night as though it was already true for me. I knew nothing about praying as a nine year old, but I did know how to have fun and use my imagination. So for me, using my imagination was the most enjoyable way to pray.

I got up early one Saturday morning to watch some cartoons. I found my mom up at her sewing machine. My mother was a gifted artist and seamstress, but this was unusual for her to be up so early sewing on a Saturday morning. She was hiding what she was doing at the sewing machine. Finally, with a little persistence on my part, I saw that she was sewing some maternity pants, the old-fashioned kind with the stretchy elastic material in the abdominal area. My eyes widened as I realized what this meant. I was ecstatic! My mother looked at me with a kind smile and she said, "You know this is all your fault!" From that point on I knew that prayer was real, and there was a force, called God, in the universe that was bigger than myself.

At nine years old I was not aware of the ancient teachings on how to pray. I just did what was natural for me. I used my *imagination*. I *felt* how delightful it would be to have a baby in the house and I *knew* for sure God would answer my prayers. Jesus put it this way:

> *Therefore I tell you, whatever you ask in prayer,*
> *believe that you have received it, and it will be yours.*
>
> –MARK 11:24

Scientist and author Gregg Braden also came to this same conclusion in his book, *The Lost Mode of Prayer*, after traveling the far corners of the world to find the most efficient form of prayer. He emphasized the importance of *feeling* what you desired was already true for you.

The secret of our lost mode of prayer is to shift our perspective of life by feeling that the miracle has already happened and our prayers have been answered. Now we have the opportunity to bring this wisdom into our lives as prayers of gratitude for what already exists, rather than asking for our prayers to be answered.

–GREGG BRADEN, AUTHOR, SCIENTIST

The perfect way to pray comes easily to a child because they are natural imaginers. Their ability to use the power and the fun of *imagination* is untarnished. They have not yet been told that they should get serious in life and quit that daydreaming!

I was already in gratitude when I prayed, because I knew I would be heard. I had confidence in my prayers, because my mother always told us kids that God listens to children's prayers more than to any other prayers. I'm not sure where my mom got that, and of course, the divine is equal in all beings no matter what their earthly age is. I think what she might have meant is that children have less resistance than adults, which allows their desires to manifest easily. I also feel to tap into imagination is a very powerful tool in prayer, intention, and manifesting. And children have strong healthy imaginations.

Most people get down on their knees and pray when they are in dire circumstances. They wait until they are desperate and experiencing great suffering and lack. This is exactly when we can't reach God. We are on a totally different frequency than the high frequency of love; we are on the desperate frequency. So get on the frequency of love and gratitude to get your prayers answered. And remember pray as though it is already true for you, *feel* what it would be like if it were already true.

Through prayer and meditation, we realize and feel the underlying oneness that permeates all that is. Through prayer we are communicating with the Oneness we call God. Per the quote at the beginning of this section, let's all join John Lennon and be dreamers (use our imagination) so the *world can live as One.*

A Prayer for Strength

This is the prayer I wrote to help me through the loss of Sal, I hope you may find it helpful for any loss you may be experiencing.

I ask for continued strength as I walk this path of healing and growth. May I grow more compassionate, empathetic, and loving, not in spite of my grief, loss, and experience, but because of them. Thank you Infinite Spirit for my life, because it is, and continues to be truly blessed. May I honor this and all moments as sacred and trust that there is a divine order to the universe that I cannot always comprehend. May I trust in the process of healing. May it teach me as I surrender to the truths revealed and may I open my heart to love more widely and boldly than I ever imagined possible. Omen, Peace, Amen

Affirmations and Mantras

Words saturated with sincerity, conviction, faith, and intuition are like highly explosive vibration bombs, which, when set off, shatter the rocks of difficulties and create the change desired.

–Paramahansa Yogananda

Affirmations are short statements spoken with conviction and truth. Many believe that affirmations are New Age or trendy. But this is not true. The yogis were doing affirmations over three thousand years ago. Paramahansa Yogananda was one of the first yogis from India to come to America. He came in the 1920s and was teaching affirmations to America a hundred years ago. You can use other people's affirmations or you can write your own. When you write your own, it is best if they are in present tense, positive, specific, and personal. Make sure you feel comfortable with the affirmation and that you also feel passionate about the affirmation. When you resonate with your affirmation it will be more effective.

Here are two of my favorite affirmations from Yogananda. These have been very effective in my life.

—*I go forth in perfect faith, with the power of omnipresent good: to bring me what I want at the time that I want it.*

—*I am Changeless, I am the Infinite. I am not a little mortal being with bones to break, a body that will perish. I am the deathless, changeless, Infinite.*

I like the first one because it covers just about everything and the second one reminds us what we most need to know.

You will find many different techniques for mastering the practice of affirmations. In the yogic tradition it is recommended to repeat an affirmation loudly and then in a regular voice and then in a whisper and lastly, within your mind. In other ancient traditions, it has been taught to silently repeat the affirmation in your mind throughout the day. The belief is that an affirmation will sink into the subconscious mind, and one will see the desired changes. The New Age teachers recommend writing down affirmations and posting them in places you regularly inhabit or use, like the bathroom on the mirror, or on the refrigerator door so that you can be reminded of them often. Or to just write then down in a journal over and over again, until you fill up several pages. There are many techniques and several books have been written on the power of affirmations. I invite you to experiment and see what works best for you. For me personally, doing all of the above works, but what I found is most important, is to say your affirmation with conviction and feel that it is already true. Much in the same way you do when you pray. After all, the two are very closely related. An affirmation is just a short, concise intention that you infuse with passion and the power of concentrated repetition.

The scientific reason for repeating mantras and affirmations is because our subconscious mind, which is about 95% of our mind, is formed from the last trimester to around six years of age. The theta brain waves are mostly used at that time, making children little sponges that literally download everything they hear. These thoughts are hardwired into our subconscious minds and are very difficult to change. However, affirmation, if used with strong concentration, have been known to break past limiting beliefs from social conditioning, even from childhood.

For example, if you heard the phrase, *money doesn't grow on trees and there is not enough,* most likely you will grow up with a scarcity attitude and it may be hard for you to feel abundance with anything, especially money. To learn more about this I suggest reading Bruce Lipton's book, *Biology of Belief*.

Affirmations are often used for healing from many different traumas. Healing from loss and grief can be helped through using affirmations. When we have experienced a deep loss in our life, our thoughts can turn very negative and feel very heavy. As a result, we can feel mentally drained and physically exhausted. Affirmations can help transform our negative thoughts into more soothing, positive thoughts.

After you have felt your emotions and feelings fully from the loss of your loved one, you do not need to dwell in suffering. I realize this is easier said than done. Be patient with yourself, have compassion for yourself, and do not judge yourself. Stay with your practice.

If you are conscious of your thoughts, then you will be able to recognize if your thoughts are negative and repetitive. If you want to have a better state of mind and get your energy back, affirmations can help. It is probably best to use your own words, unless you find one that says it better than you could and it resonates with you. Here are some positive affirmations that may resonate with you.

—I know for sure, Love knows no death.

—My loved one would never want me to dwell in depression over his/her transition.

—I let go of my sadness and hold on to the love and gratitude I have for _____.

—I let go of all negative and fear-based thoughts.

—I know that in truth we are all connected to each other; I am never alone.

—I am loved beyond measure, connected, protected, and divinely guided, always!

—My peace of mind is essential to my well-being. Feeling good is good for me and everyone around me.

—I think positively; it feels good and allows my future to unfold with beauty and love.

—I dwell in love and gratitude

—I am whole.

—I accept all that life presents to me, even when I cannot change it.

—I let my heart open, I am safe.

—New strengths and insights are coming to me all the time as I move through life with ease.

—I use all life challenges as opportunities for growth and expansion.

—I trust in the divine order of the universe.

—I am free to explore, expand, and experience the infinite potential unfolding from within me.

—Please forgive me, thank you, I love you (one of my favorites; simple and powerful, derived from the ancient Hawaiian healers, this prayer/affirmation is called *Ho'oponopono*; there are many books you can buy to learn more about this powerfully effective affirmation/prayer)

The use of a mantra, or prayer word, allows us to channel our energy toward our divine nature. When negative mind states arise such as anxiety, anger, or fear, we can use the energy of these emotions in a positive way by introducing the mantra into the mental field. The "fire" or energy of the emotion then becomes a transforming fire instead of a destructive fire.

–ELLEN GRACE O'BRIAN, AUTHOR, TEACHER

It write briefly of the manta here, as it was already described in the meditation section. The mantam is closely related to affirmations because they are also used in a repetitive manner. Mantras are sacred words of power. Mantras are used in meditation to train the mind to be single-focused. Mantras are usually only one or two words and are repeated with each, in and out breath during meditation. Mantas can be several words or one word, like love. An excellent book to read to acquire a better understanding of mantras is by reading the book by Eknath Easwaran, a past meditation teacher at UC Berkeley, called, *The Mantram Handbook.*

Intention

Intention appears to be something akin to a tuning fork, causing the tuning forks of other things in the universe to resonate at the same frequency.

–Lynne McTaggert, Authority on Intention,
Author, Researcher

You can set an intention word anytime you want; I like to set intention words at the beginning of the New Year. Intention words are usually only one word and are meaningful to the person who sets it. An intention word, like a mantra, is a powerful, sacred word. You can choose the word that best describes the soul quality you would like to manifest in your life.

I like to do this practice at the beginning of January every year with my students, family, and friends. It is more powerful to do intentions with others, but is not necessary. I keep everyone's intention word, which is handwritten by them on an index card, and placed it in a basket in the middle of the meditation studio. Each week in class, we energize all of the intention words through meditation, prayer, and sound. It is important to write down your intention word and place it where you will periodically see it. You can write your intention on an index card, with colored pencils, and do some artwork to make your intention word more meaningful and special to you. You can also write it in a journal and describe why you picked this particular word.

Intention words work differently than setting a New Year's resolution. The New Year's resolution typically does not work. It is usually something physical, like losing weight. So you are working with matter to matter. Which is slower, denser, and harder to work with. Intentions are usually soul qualities you would like to bring into your life. For example, love, gratitude, peace, and abundance. They are not material-based. When working on intentions you are working with energy, which can manifest much quicker. The intention you set will most likely find you when it is energy to energy. It is fun and effective to set your word in a special intention group meditation.

Lynne McTaggart's book, *The Power of Eight: Harnessing the Miraculous Energies of a Small Group to Heal Others, Your Life, and the*

World, will give you the research and examples of how powerful it is to set intentions with others. In her book she teaches how to get a group and set and manifest intentions together. The number of the participants in the group is not strict, it does not have to be a group of eight, it can be any number, but has to be more than one. The important part is to form a small group of people and set an intention for one of them. The most fascinating finding in her research is that all of those holding the intention will also benefit as much as the person receiving the intention!

Yoga and Movement

Yoga is about clearing away whatever is in us that prevents our living in the most full and whole way. With yoga, we become aware of how and where we are restricted—in body, mind, and heart—and how gradually to open and release these blockages.

–CYBELE TOMLINSON, AUTHOR

Yoga works on all levels of our being—physical, mental, emotional, and spiritual. It helps keep one present and flexible in body and mind. Yoga releases blockages in the body and mind, allowing for a free flow of energy throughout the body. Most people recognize the physical benefits of yoga, but often miss the greatest benefits, which are mental and spiritual. It strengthens the mind to be focused and leads one to higher awareness.

Yoga is working with mastering your life force. In the practice of yoga we are learning to direct the flow of energy in our body. Advanced yoga is not tying yourself up in knots, or standing on your head, rather it is feeling and directing our *prana*, our life force or energy, bringing that energy inward and upward. When you practice yoga you do not need to know any of this, just try it and see how you feel. When you begin, go to a class that is gentle and is led by an experienced teacher. If you want a more physically challenging class, you can find one, but make sure it is still leading you to higher awareness through your practice.

It is important to remember that yoga is meant to be a personal practice, it brings you within. It is not meant to be competitive or outward type of exercise. Through the body you are brought to an inward presence. The healthy side effects are very positive and beneficial; you will gain strength, flexibility, balance, and peace of mind. You will lose weight and anxiety and your cortisol levels in the blood will decrease. Your blood pressure, cholesterol, and heart rate will also stabilize. However, the real purpose of yoga is to help prepare the body for sitting meditation. The ancient sages of the East created and used yoga to exercise the body and still the mind. This way it was possible to sit for long periods of time in stillness, providing a deep meditation. Yoga itself can be practiced as a moving meditation.

We learn to go to the breath in yoga to stay grounded in presence and to contract and then relax our muscles. We go to the breath in yoga as we are stretching to our personal boundaries on the mat. Later we take this practice into life. We practice deep breathing and we relax through our personal limitations to get deeper in reaching our goals, instead of pushing to attain our goals. In yoga you take all that you practice on the mat—presence, acceptance, forgiveness, conscious breathing, relaxation, and gratitude—into your daily life. You practice letting go of comparisons, competition, stress, and anxiety. The practice goes far beyond the mat. I found the practice of yoga to be a constant in my life that keeps me healthy, calm, grounded, centered, and content.

Any movement that leads to presence and health is wonderful. It can be dance, qigong, tai chi, hiking, swimming, running, skiing, or even just walking. The ways to get movement in our lives are bountiful. Studies show that exercise is one of the best things you can do to keep a strong, healthy mind. It has been shown to increase happiness and diminish or even eliminate depression. Exercise is the closest thing we have to the fountain of youth, keeping us lean, fit, energetic, and with glowing skin. Keep your body moving in a safe and effective way. Stay consistent with your practice. Keep it simple and enjoyable. Don't beat yourself up with exercise, it catches up with you when you over stress your body. Be kind to your body and enjoy moving it in ways that empower you.

Breath

Breathing in, I calm my body and mind. Breathing out, I smile. Dwelling in the present moment I know this is the only moment.

–THICH NHAT HANH, MONK, AUTHOR, PEACE LEADER

I have had many students who have been injured and cannot do the physical yoga practice, but will sit and breathe with the yoga class. The breathing exercises alone bring healing and harmony to their bodies, minds, and soul. In yoga and meditation as well as many other similar practices, we learn to breathe correctly. Deep belly breathing is practiced, engaging the diaphragm to allow more oxygen to enter the lungs. To take in more oxygen you learn to expand the abdomen outward on the *in* breath and allow the belly to sink back into the spine on the *out* breath. We learn to breathe deep from the abdomen and not shallow from the chest and throat. Deep belly breathing slows down our heart rate and brain waves; shallow breathing speeds up our heart rate and our brain waves.

In my early twenties, I worked in the field of biofeedback; I was a registered dental hygienist working in a clinic that dealt primarily with patients who suffered from severe temporomandibular joint disorder, also known as TMJ (jaw joint) pain. These patients were in tremendous pain from either clenching or grinding their teeth, unconsciously. First we hooked them up to biofeedback machines, and then we would teach them to relax by instructing them to breathe properly, as described above.

Within minutes, the breath is capable of transforming the inner workings of the body. With simple deep diaphragmatic breathing, the heart rate slows down, the blood pressure lowers, muscles relax, the brain waves slow down from beta to alpha and theta, and now we also know the cortisol levels decrease to ensure healthy functioning of the body. When patients are hooked up to biofeedback machines, one can visibly observe many of these bodily changes. The patients quickly learned how to breathe correctly to eliminate the habit of clenching and grinding from stress, with the advantage of seeing how the breathing technique positively affects and releases the tension and anxiety they are experiencing.

It was at this time that I became even more intrigued with meditation, yoga, and the breath and the role that these practices play in health and wellness. Simple deep breathing can heal many aliments caused by stress. Proper breathing can be one of the most effective medicines, and it is free and with us all the time. We just need to remember to breathe correctly. To breathe deeply, slowly, and more rhythmically from the belly.

Health and Well-Being

I don't understand why asking people to eat a well-balanced vegetarian diet is considered drastic, while it is medically conservative to cut people open and put them on cholesterol lowering drugs for the rest of their lives.

–DEAN ORNISH, MD, AUTHOR, WELLNESS EXPERT

There is so much information out on the importance of exercise and diet that I will not go into much detail here. I will briefly present the latest information on nutrition. And also on how our state of consciousness affects our mental, emotional, spiritual, and physical health. It is a known fact that all of these components are connected and are basically one. Our mind and body are one living organism, intertwined and created for thriving. If one is not cared for and not well, the other will soon follow.

In Dr. Dean Ornish's latest book, *Undo It! 'How Simple Lifestyle Changes Can Reverse Most Chronic Diseases*, he goes into detail on how loving more can save your life. He wrote this book with his wife, Anne Ornish; the two of them have been working in the field of disease and lifestyle change for over forty years. He has proven that lifestyle has more of an impact than most medicines in reversing most chronic diseases. The four components of his program, as practiced in many hospitals around the country are; eat well, move more, stress less, and love more.

Dr. Ornish has a system that is scientifically proven to reverse heart disease without drugs or surgery. His work is mainstream and has been out for forty years, but for some reason, many people seem to ignore it or not believe it is possible to heal and reverse chronic disease, through lifestyle. Many people rather take a pill and hope that the magic pill will fix them.

Most of us know that proper nutrition, exercise, and dealing wisely with stress will keep the doctor away. But not everyone realizes that loving more keeps us healthy. How well you love others and yourself, and how well you are loved, are important factors in your overall health. Loneliness, depression, and isolation are factors that contribute to poor health and lead to chronic illness. People need people, more than ever now. It is a well-known fact that suicide rates are on the rise. It has been deomstrated over and over again through scientific research that love heals and loneliness and isolation compromise and can even destroy our health. (For more on connection see the Connection section coming up.)

Another book I recommend for the current studies on health and longevity is the book, *The Longevity Diet*, by Dr. Valter Longo. This book focuses more on nutrition, intermittent fasting, mimicking fasting, and exercise. It teaches you to eat in a way that can give you an abundance of energy and more importantly activate and regenerate your stem cells to fight diseases and slow aging. Dr. Longo recommends a plant-based diet and intermittent fasting. He recommends eating fish two to three times a week for those who are sixty-five years old and above and those prone to weight loss.

I remember hearing Jack LaLanne, the original fitness guru, when I was just a child, say, *If it grew on a tree or out of the earth, it is good for you.* He had it right way back in the sixties. It is actually just common sense. We can't go wrong by eating organic fresh vegetables, fruits, grains, legumes, nuts, and spices grown in nutrient rich soil. Juicing organic fruits and veggies is an easy and delicious way to get the recommended ten servings a day of vegetables. However, according to Ayurveda, raw food is not good for most people. I have studied and practiced Ayurveda health practices. It looks at the individual and treats each person individually according to their *doshas*. It takes into account your *dosha*, which includes your body type, your temperament, the environment, and many other factors. It is an extensive science to study, yet it is worth the time to learn the beneficial practices. Physicians, such as Deepak Chopra and Vijay Jain who have studied both Western and Eastern medicine and have blended these sciences are excellent for helping patients to have access to the best of both traditional Western medicine and Eastern medicine. I have undertaken several sessions of *panchakarma* with Dr. Vijay to detoxify my body and mind and to prevent illnesses. These week long sessions include meditation, breathwork, yoga, health education, and Ayurvedic medical treatments including daily massage. I always leave feeling rejuvenated and energized. I feel the time and money invested for these sessions are well worth it for the preventive and healing aspects it provides. Dr. Vijay is based in Florida; you can find more information at www.mindbodywellness.com.

For optimum wellness, I recommend regular massages and acupuncture as an effective way to prevent disease and promote wellness. Benjamin

Franklin was wise to have said, *An Ounce of Prevention Is Worth A Pound of Cure*. He coined this timeless phrase in 1736 and it holds true today for health and wellness.

Our thoughts and our state of mind have a profound impact on our overall health and well-being. So many books have been written throughout the years on the importance of positive thinking and how our thoughts and our current state of consciousness have an effect on our lives. Ancient sages have been teaching this for over three thousand years. The classic book written by James Allen, *As a Man Thinketh*, was published in 1903. There are many other leading thought teachers throughout the last two centuries, teaching of the importance of your thoughts and how they affect our lives. Some of these teachers were Dale Carnegie, born in 1888, Napoleon Hill, born in 1883, Paramahansa Yogananda, born in 1893, and Earl Nightingale, born in 1921, as well as Catherine Ponder, born in 1927, who wrote, *The Dynamic Laws of Prosperity*. In truth, throughout recorded history, the importance of our thoughts have also been taught by Lazu, Buddha, Jesus, and most of the saints and sages of ancient times.

When you realize you are manifesting constantly through your thoughts whether you are aware of it or not, it is a first step in the awakening process. It is wise to manifest consciously through positive thoughts. But to master the mind, you need to practice awareness. Much of this book is about awareness; revisit the sections on presence and meditation if you would like more on awareness.

Energy Medicine

As daily life pulls us further from our natural rhythms, Energy Medicine reminds us of who we are and reconnects us with our deepest nature.

–DONNA EDEN, AUTHOR, HEALER

When I use the term, "energy medicine," I simply mean that when energy is flowing freely through the body as it was meant to be, it can improve our physical, mental, emotional, and spiritual well-being. When energy is flowing freely through our bodies and is not stuck or obstructed, or flowing in the wrong direction, our health improves. You can compare it with how important this is for the blood flowing through the body and how disease is formed when our circulation is obstructed, clotted, or goes into reverse flow.

Preventive practices of energy medicine consist of movements and exercises that keep us healthy and strong. These would include such practices as yoga, tai chi, qigong, Donna Eden's five-minute routine, Yogananda's energization routine, and many other movement practices. Anything that moves energy in our bodies in a positive way for well-being can be considered a form of energy medicine. And since we are made of energy, practices such as meditation, mantras, prayers, positive thoughts, EFT, sound therapy, light therapy, and endless bodywork specialties are also considered energy medicine. These practices help release blockages and open the meridians (pathways in the body) for energy to flow freely.

I do believe that energy medicine will be used more as the medical field advances. There needs to be more research and studies on how energy medicine works; however, it may be the wave of the future for healing. It works much faster and with fewer side effects than traditional chemical medicines, although chemical drugs at this time have their place in medicine.

Dr. Joe Dispenza and Lynne McTaggert are both experiencing many spontaneous healings in their workshops and retreats, from their work with meditation, intention, and coherence between the heart and brain. As I mentioned above, these are practices that work with energy. Dr. Dispenza has his students hooked up to medical diagnostic machines, so that he and other scientist can observe the spontaneous changes occurring in the brain and body during certain meditative practices.

Energy medicine can help with grief, and improve health in general. It helps to keep your energy levels high and prevents illnesses in the body that can arise from depression and low energy. Many times energy will heal an individual when nothing else works.

Preventive energy medicine practices (from Donna Eden's exercises or others) can be incorporated into your yoga practice or whatever you have chosen to do as your daily movement practice or all by itself. Again, it works with the energy in the body for wellness and for either prevention or elimination of disease in the body.

I like to practice Donna Eden's five-minute routine. All you have to do to learn this is go on YouTube or buy one of her books. I also like to do Paramahansa Yogananda's energization exercises which can be Googled; there is also an app for it, called Energization. These energizations practices have been around for as long as yoga and have proven to keep your immune system strong and your body and mind healthy.

Emotional Freedom Technique

EFT releases healing hormones which activates the bodies natural ability to heal itself.

–Lisa Rankin, MD, Author

I found that using emotional freedom technique (also called EFT or tapping) as a tool for transcending grief and coming deeper into acceptance and presence is very effective for me. EFT is great to use for almost anything. I have found it very effective when I am feeling anxiety. It is so simple to use. Many people just call it tapping; you tap on certain meridians in the body. As mention previously, meridians are pathways, which energy/ life force, also know as chi in Chinese medicine can flow through our bodies. You do not need to understand exactly how EFT works to reap the quick results.

There are many good books to read to get a further understanding of EFT. Gary Craig created the EFT, so reading his books or watching his videos would be a great place to start. I would suggest watching a YouTube video by Nick Ortner, who wrote, *The Tapping Solution.* You can easily learn how to practice EFT from watching his videos. Jessica Ortner, his sister, is also very good to learn from and an author on tapping for weight loss. Jessica also has many excellent YouTube on EFT.

The fact that it is so simple to do, may make you think it could not possibly work for moving through grief, but it does. There are also many certified practitioners you can go to for therapy with EFT, if you do not yet feel comfortable performing it on yourself. I have found it to be very effective, but do not take my word, try it out for yourself. It only takes a few minutes to perform at the end of my meditation practice.

Journaling

I want to go on living even after my death! And therefore I am grateful to God for giving me this gift, this possibility of developing myself and of writing, of expressing all that is in me. I can shake off everything if I write; my sorrows disappear, my courage is reborn.

–ANNE FRANK, AUTHOR

I have found journaling to be a helpful practice for many reasons. But the most important reason is that writing helps you find what is deep inside you that wants to come out and be heard and acknowledged. Journaling is just for yourself; it's like dancing or singing with nobody watching. Don't be concerned with punctuation and correct grammar. Write straight from your heart and you just might be surprised at what comes out. You can always decide later if you want to share it.

Another benefit of the written word, is that when you write down your intentions and goals in your journal, they most likely will manifest easily, even when you have forgotten all about them. It is good practice to write down goals at the beginning of the year and let go of them, it's fine to forget about them. When you revisit your goals at the end of the year, you may be surprised at how easily some of them have manifested. After experiencing this phenomenon myself, I saw a book titled, *Write it Down, Make it Happen,* by Henriette Klauser. Seeing this book validated my own experience. I bought the book because I loved the title. Honestly the title is all you need.

For example, my intention for writing this book is purely to help others through challenges that life presents to all of us. One of the beneficial side effects of taking on this endeavor was that I have gained insights and clarity on my own healing journey that were not evident to me before I wrote this book. This was a nice surprise which I'm grateful for.

Nature

I only went out for a walk and finally concluded to stay out until sundown, for going out, I found, was really going in.

–John Muir, Author, Naturalist

When I am in nature is when I feel the closest to God. I have had some of my best meditations in nature, whether it is the forest, the seaside, the mountains, the dessert, or even my own backyard. We lose ourselves in the great outdoors. We feel more connected in nature than we do indoors. The yogis remind us that there is much more *prana* available outdoors. If you remember from the previous section on the inner body, *prana* means life force. This life force that can be described as an aliveness that runs through all of us, all living creatures, and all around us, serves as a bridge from form to formlessness, from body to spirit. As the quote by John Muir above tells us, a walk in nature leads us to a journey within, again from without to within, from body to spirit.

There is a phenomenon, which originated in Japan and has become quite popular all over the world, called, "forest bathing." Forest bathing is when we move slowly or even sit in the forest amongst the trees and take in the beauty of the forest, the smells, the sights, the sounds, and so forth. It also includes touching and hugging the trees. It has been shown through science that our bodies and minds are healed and rejuvenated from this practice of just "being" in the forest. The book *Forest Bathing* by Dr. Qing Li has a wealth of fascinating scientific information to demonstrate the many healing benefits of the forest. There are many negative ions in the forest air, especially if there is a stream or waterfall. Ions are charged particles in the air. Dr. Qing Li states, "Negative ions have energizing and refreshing effects, and help to increase mental clarity and our sense of well-being."

In January of 2013, ten months before Sal's passing, I spent five days on a silent retreat on the North Island of New Zealand. The retreat was located in the mountainous region of Tairua, and the Buddhist retreat center was called Te Moata. I was not expecting a silent retreat to be going on when I arrived, but it was the only way to stay there and I thought, since it's all in divine order, it might be perfect for me and it was! We meditated all day and also in the evening. We had breaks for meals and free time after lunch, but we were to remain in silence.

After lunch, I went for a hike up in the steep forested mountain range that loomed over the monastery. The monks gave you large bright plastic whistles to take in case you got lost; it was strung on a thick string so you could wear it around your neck. And they had tied a small strand of rope around several trees so you could find your way back. They were not very obvious so you had to be very alert and present to notice them. I made my way through overgrown, feathery silver-green Ponga ferns and came across several flowing streams with fallen branches that acted as flimsy bridges to carefully tip-toe across. It was a warm sunny day so I enjoyed taking my shoes and socks off and waded around in the fresh water pools. I had to climb up several handmade ladders to get higher up in the mountain. As I continued my hike up to higher elevations, the terrain began to change from ferns and small trees to larger trees.

As I climbed higher up the mountains of Te Moata, I came across a charming rustic little log cabin. There was a wooded sign attached to the cabin near the front door and engraved in the wood, it read, Kauri Cabin. I knew that when the Te Moata Retreat was not holding programs, they rented out cabins. I thought I'd see if the door was open and get an idea of what the cabins are like, in case I ever get back here. As soon as I entered, an adventurous and magical feeling came over me, in this sweet cabin. It was the way the whole journey through the forest felt, but now it was amplified by finding this lone cabin in the middle of nowhere high up on the mountain. The first thing I saw as I walked in was an incredible azure blue, as I looked closer I realize this brilliant blue was the sea below the mountain, meeting the sky. From the outside you had no idea that the sea was just beyond the forest! The cabin had round windows with stain glass of colorful birds and butterflies. The floor was wood and the cabin was extremely simple with one double bed covered with a worn handmade quilt and big velvet pillows of jeweled colors. There was a small kitchen with a wood burning stove and nearby was a cardboard box filled with twigs and small branches. There was a cozy living room, with a rocking chair. In the corner facing the view was a meditation cushion with a small handmade wood altar. But, what I found most intriguing in this cabin was placed on the altar, which was the true treasure of the cabin. It was a very small thin book, titled, *Dhammapada*, with the subtitle, *The Sayings of the Buddha*. It was obvious that this cabin was vacant, so I took my time in the cabin enjoying this delightful space. I read the sayings in the little Buddha book. I have never studied the Buddha before, other than reading about Siddhartha in high school. But, every saying seemed to have been written just for me. I also felt the spirit of these teachings and felt a close connection with the Buddha that I had never felt before.

Here I was, at a Buddhist retreat in the mountains of New Zealand. It was the first time in my life I had ever traveled solo to a foreign country or actually anywhere. I welcomed the adventure! A friend back home comes to this retreat center often and spoke highly of the beauty and energy here at Te Moata. It felt safe for my first time traveling alone to be in a retreat center, and it turned out to be one of the best experiences of my life.

I knew I had to get back to the retreat center for the afternoon meditation. I closed up the Kauri Cabin and was in gratitude for the whole experience of the woods, waterfalls, and this sweet mysterious cabin. I hoped I could find my way back to the meditation room at the retreat center below. As I was looking for my way back, I was drawn to a grove of old growth giant Kauri trees. This area of New Zealand has the enormous Kauri trees, which are some of the largest and longest living trees in the world. I was fortunate to come upon a whole grove of them, they were towering over me, and I felt so small standing amongst these giant, majestic forces of life in the mossy green forest. I decided, I just needed to sit for a few minutes in their presence. As soon as I sat comfortably cross-legged at the base of a gigantic Kauri tree, the stillness of these angelic trees swept over me and infused me with a deep peace that transported me into one of the deepest meditations I have ever experienced. As I sank deeper and deeper into alert stillness and tranquil silence, I heard the voice of responsibility saying *you need to get back to the group for the afternoon meditation*. But then the quieter voice of spirit said, *this is what you are here for; the Divine comes in unexpected ways do not interrupt this deep stillness, rather relax and go deeper.* So I let the voice of wisdom guide me as I surrendered even deeper into the stillness and silence that was slowly engulfing me.

Hours had passed when I came out of this blissful meditation. I calmly followed my instincts and was led by my sense of direction back to the retreat center. The afternoon session had ended; I found my teacher inside, closing up the room. I explained to him what happened and profusely apologized. To my surprised, he was very happy for me; he explained that even though he lived in England now, he grew up here in New Zealand. When he was a young man, he worked hard in a job, he did not enjoy, but he wanted to make his parents and others happy so he stuck it out. The one thing that kept him grounded and centered was coming to the forest of the Kauri trees on the weekends and backpacking in the forest and mountains. It was the Kauri trees that awakened him to live the life he now lives. He loves his life now and would never go back to the life he previously led. He spends all his time teaching meditation through silent retreats all over the world. He completely understood and had also experienced the power of the Kauri trees, leading him home to his true Essence.

Now as I look back at this experience, I know that being in nature was key to this transcendental experience. Walking in the forest, I was led to feeling so relaxed, present, and grateful for the beauty of this mountainous forest. *Because of walking in nature*, I easily opened to receiving the gift of spirit through the Kauri trees. Nature guides us to know ourselves on a deeper level, to feel loved, to feel gratitude, relaxed, open, and present. Make it a habit to spend time in nature often.

This silent retreat was led through the Insight Meditation group, also known as Vipassanā meditation. There was a point in the retreat where they asked us to pick one person who loves us very intensely and who we love intensely. We were to connect on a spiritual level with that person. I picked Sal. Now I know, it was no accident that I chose Sal, it was only ten months before his transition. This practice helped me later on to connect with Sal's formless Self. And Sal loved so intensely! Or I should say *loves* so intensely!

CHAPTER TEN:

Mindset

Faith and Trust ~ Connection ~ Environment ~ Humor ~ Gratitude ~ Kindness ~ The Power of Forgiveness ~ Self Love ~ Know Thyself

The mindset is the cornerstone to achieving a successful life, which I define as a life filled with peace, passion, purpose, and contentment. The mindset is not something we do; it is what we become with practice.

Faith and Trust

Let faith be the bridge you build to overcome evil and welcome good.

–OPRAH, TV PRODUCER, PHILANTHROPIST

I have always intuitively known that all that happens to us is in divine order. Even though life may feel and look chaotic for us, there is an underlying order to all of it that we just can't see. Many times in our lives we get clarity later to the significance of events that happened earlier, which at that time make no sense. And sometimes certain things may never make sense to us; this is where trust comes in. I don't suggest blind faith here; I feel *faith* is more of a *deep intuitive knowing*. If something rings true to you, it probably is. Have you ever felt the chills when either you or someone you know says something that feels so right? I felt the chills and experienced ah-ha moments often after Sal passed as I was speaking to others; it was almost as if Sal was speaking through me and I loved the profound clarity I was getting and sharing. It was almost as if I was an instrument for truth to come through. I was blessed with the ability to be in alignment at these times with Infinite Intelligence. You can feel the difference between truth, which feels like an ah-ha moment, and lies, which feels like an ache in the gut or heart. Learn to feel your body's response—the body doesn't lie.

When I first learned about the effects of positive thinking, I tested it out for myself. I was working in a profession that had served me well, but I was ready to get out of it, and yet I felt stuck because of the good salary and security it gave me. I noticed that this feeling of being stuck was making my workday unpleasant. When I decided to go to work and be in gratitude about all the good things the job provided for me, everything changed. Before I knew it, I was working full-time in my dream job. Simply because I changed my attitude. I had a *belief* that if I went into gratitude, it could possibly transform my work into what I hoped for. By having an experience of what I expected could be true, I was able to build faith. Faith is not blind, it is not believing in God because the official at your place of worship said to. No, you need to *experience* a glimpse of the truth to have faith. Sometimes people think belief and faith are the same thing. However, they are not, when you have a belief and it is converted into direct experience, it becomes faith. And a belief is a thought we have thought over and over and hold to be true. In reality it may or may not be true. What is true for one person may not be true for another, because of different beliefs.

So if we can hold the possibility and have a belief that our loved ones are actually here with us, it opens up the door to infinite possibilities, like unexpected signs from them that make us laugh out loud, while at the same time our eyes tear up from the knowing that they are here playing with us, what a miracle! But a belief without experience is useless if you don't test it out and live by it. If you have had one sign, it is enough to build faith. When we directly experience a sign from our deceased loved ones or an answer to a prayer, it is not blind faith. Rather, it builds faith, it is a knowing, a trusting, and an intuitive guidance that we go with even when the reasoning voice is saying, no. Faith is an intuitive conviction of truth.

I had an experience that was much like a near-death experience that forever made me trust in the divine order of the universe. I was assisting Gurudev, Amrit Desai, in San Francisco, with a yoga nidra workshop at Yoga Tree. Gurdev, is a beloved teacher and yoga master from India who created the Amrit Yoga Institute in Florida. I got very deep in a yoga nidra meditation session led by Gurdev. In this meditation I went into a very vivid lucid dream, I was completely aware and conscious in the dream. I saw my life in review and received a full understanding of how each event in my life, the good and the so-called bad, were given to me for my own personal growth. The part of the experience that stood out the most was the most horrible thing that happened to me at that time, losing my brother, Michael, in a senseless hate crime. (this has already been described in Part I) In this meditation I realized that Michaels murder, had a profound, positive affect in my life. This yoga nidra session showed me beyond question, that life is always here to lead us to awakening to our true essence, for growth and expansion of consciousness. This experience demonstrated that all is in a divine order, beyond what our tiny human brains can reason.

This experience confirmed my *belief* that all is in divine order, to a *direct knowing* that all is in divine order. I don't need faith or trust that all is in divine order, I know it, but it was faith and trust that led me to this knowing, and now it is a rock-solid truth for me—***All is in divine order.***

Connection

When we focus on ourselves, our world contracts - but when we focus on others, our world expands. Our own problems drift to the periphery of the mind and so seem smaller, and we increase our capacity for connection - or compassionate action.

–DANIEL GOLEMAN, AUTHOR

As humans beings we need connection for our souls to thrive, as much as we need food and water to nourish our physical bodies. The need for connection is primal in human beings. Whether we realize it or not, our need for connection with one another and with our community is vital for a healthy body, mind, and soul. There are numerous studies which demonstrate this truth.

I have always instinctively known that to give love and receive love is the greatest experience we can have, and our love for one another is what life is all about. If you are feeling lonely or isolated, take action to connect with others. Nourish yourself with connections to other human beings. Another way to nourish connection is to get a pet; most pets love us unconditionally. There is so much we can learn from our furry friends. There are numerous studies that demonstrate the health benefits of pets on their owners. It has been shown that elderly people living with pets have longer, happier, and healthier lives.

If you are feeling lonely and isolated, begin to give what you desire. You can start by simply smiling at strangers you pass who might need a bit of compassion, being kind to the store clerk by looking them in the eye as you say thank you for their help, opening the door for someone, or giving up your seat to someone who needs it more. These simple acts of kindness and connection can make others feel valued and in return will bring you more of the connection you desire and enjoy. These simple acts can help you develop the ability and confidence to reach out to connect with friends and family. Let go of resentment and give yourself the gift of connection.

Most of us feel that we are part of something much larger than ourselves, we are connected to each other in a very real way, a way that cannot be seen, but can be *felt*. As the ancient Sufi mystic, Rumi, said in the thirteenth century, *Do not feel lonely, the entire universe is within you.* When you learn to feel this enormous connection, that Rumi speaks of here, you will feel your connection with passed loved ones as well as your connection to Source. But you still need a good supply of connection to family and friends as you are still living on this earth. To put it simply, people need people!

Environment

A person's health isn't generally a reflection of genes,
but how their environment is influencing them.

–BRUCE LIPTON, CELLULAR BIOLOGIST, AUTHOR

The environment we place ourselves in is very important for our outlook on life as well as our health. When I say environment, I am referring to not only our physical surroundings, like where we live, but also our social environment, the people we surround ourselves with, the books and movies we consume, and where and how we spend our time.

Napoleon Hill, Yogananda, Bruce Lipton and many other new thought leaders, have agreed that environment is stronger than willpower. For example if an alcoholic wanted to quit drinking, but worked as a bartender, spent his free time with friends who took him wine tasting, and took a vacation to Germany for the Octoberfest, it would be very difficult for one to refrain from alcohol.

In much the same way, if one is in the healing process from a deep loss and is prone to depression, it would not be conducive to the healing process to be watching violent movies, reading books that tell stories of abusive situations, or hanging out with people who are narcissistic.

On the other hand, surrounding oneself in a calming environment, taking classes that resonate with your soul, such as art, creative writing, tai chi, and so forth, spending time in nature to revel in the beauty of our planet and traveling to nearby beautiful and peaceful places can bring the peace and harmony your soul is craving. Also, volunteering to work with and help children, animals, the homeless, or anyone else you choose can also be very helpful for healing. Being of service of any kind is one of the best environments to place yourself in for healing. Adopt a puppy or a kitten and bring that new family member into your home. Observing the way these animals love you unconditionally is one of the best ways to enhance your well-being and your home environment.

Make your home and work environment one of beauty. Create a home that is clean and uncluttered. The spaciousness will create a calming effect on you and others in your home. Have only your favorite items in your home. Donate the items you don't need or love; someone else will cherish them. Frame something you created, or your child or grandchild created, and hang it on that perfect wall space. I found that by simply moving items (furniture, wall hangings etc) around in my home gave it a fresh new ambience; I did not have to buy anything new. Think of fun, easy, and creative ways to make your home, garden, and work space your own sacred sanctuary.

I invite you to create your own space and make it your private sanctuary, no matter how simple, or small it might be. We make our environment beautiful by the way we physically decorate it, but what actually makes it sacred is what happens in that space on a regular basis, what energy is going on in your space. Everything is energy and whether you are aware of it or not, it permeates every molecule of your environment and affects the well-being of all who dwell there.

You may have noticed that once you begin to change to leading a more authentic and empowered life, your environment seems to catch up with these qualities you have become. The friends who were heavily egotistic and materially oriented seem to fall away, without any doing on your part. At first this may feel sad, especially if you are an empath, because you tend to see the good in people. And sometimes that good you are seeing isn't actually authentic! It's the wolf in sheep clothing, so stay centered in love and gratitude and those who stay near to you in the good times and the hard times are your real dear friends. Let your own guidance system lead you to an environment that feels good. Your guidance system is your emotions. So to use your guidance system, pay attention to how you feel.

Humor

Comedy can be a cathartic way to deal with personal trauma.

–ROBIN WILLIAMS, ACTOR, COMEDIAN

Crying and laughing are both excellent ways to release stress and tension in our bodies. However, there are appropriate times for both. I like to think of crying as a release and cleanse. But, humor is something that we can bathe in daily to improve our lives. There are many studies that demonstrate how humor is the best medicine to keep our immune system strong and our mental and emotional health in check. Humor also keeps us humble, especially if we have the ability to laugh at ourselves. Humor that is genuinely funny and is done without malice toward another can uplift us. A good sense of humor keeps us light, joyful, and positive.

If you have someone in your life that keeps you laughing, make sure you appreciate him or her and spend time with that person often. I am blessed to have my son Arthur, who has a great sense of humor, he keeps me laughing every day. His ability to make others laugh is a gift, and there is nothing he enjoys more than making others laugh, going to comedy shows, and being around others who have a good sense of humor and enjoy laughter. And then there is Sal, my spirit son, who keeps me laughing with all his unexpected signs, some are inspirational, but many are just funny! All of the signs are fun surprises that are delivered with unmatched creativity. I am blessed with some humorous friends in my life whom I love to be with. One way to know if you have a person in your life that is playful is to notice how you feel after you have spent time with them. This is the real test of how funny they are. If you feel lighter and uplifted, the person is truly comical, if you feel bad, they are the mean humor types, which isn't really funny.

Sometimes a pair of kittens or two puppies playing together can really be funny, another good reason to have our furry friends nearby. These days we have a choice of so many movies with all the streaming options available.

Make humor a part of your daily life by sharing time with those who make you laugh and learn from them how to offer humor to those you love. No doubt, laughter is good for your body, mind, and soul. So make sure you are finding humor somewhere in your life. As we awaken to the bigger picture of life, we ease up, let go of fear, and laugh more easily, because we are becoming lighter.

Gratitude

The most fortunate, are those who have a wonderful capacity to appreciate again and again, freshly and naively, the basic goods of life, with awe, pleasure, wonder and even ecstasy.

−Abraham Maslow, PhD, Author, Professor of Psychology

Living our lives in a state of gratitude is like living with a wise sage who continually guides us whenever we need it. Use the practice of gratitude in the same way sailors used the North Star for navigation.

In much the same way, when we feel gratitude in everyday life, it keeps us on a higher path. And if we really think about it, there is always something to be grateful for. The fact that the sun rises and the birds sing every morning is reason enough to get out of bed and be grateful for life. In truth, seeing the sunrise and hearing the birds sing is quite phenomenal.

While Sal was here on earth, I always felt so grateful to have him in my life. And when he left, that gratitude deepened. I personally found that feeling my love for Sal, and then allowing that love to lead me into appreciation for the time we had together on earth, set me in a solid state of combined love and gratitude. The hard part might be to stay in gratitude. Sometimes, after we lose someone, every little thing we see or hear can remind us of that person and we feel the hole in our heart. Again, the key is awareness of your thoughts and feelings, going quickly back to gratitude can help us get back on track and prevent us from dropping down into sadness. And as an added bonus, gratitude helps to keep us connected with our loved one.

I was already in the habit of practicing gratitude before Sal made his transition. I have had a gratitude journal for years and taught classes on the importance of gratitude. When you write down what you are grateful for, it seems to take it to a higher level. When you look at the beauty of this planet and feel grateful, it feels good. When you share what you are grateful for with others, it amps up the power of feeling gratitude.

When I lost Sal, friends and family showed their love by sending cards, flowers, donations, and presents, and came over to bring us food and give us hugs. I felt extremely grateful. The kind acts of others helped me tremendously. However, if we do not appreciate these acts, because we are too self-absorbed in our sorrow, we miss out on gratitude. And if that happened to you, do not feel bad, it is never too late to find gratitude. We are human beings and we are not *always* going to be in gratitude and that's ok, be easy on yourself. When you are in states of anger and depression, it is almost impossible to feel gratitude. You will move out of those states quicker if you could practice even a little bit of gratitude. I do recommend a gratitude journal. Make it just for you and take five minutes on some mornings to write down what you feel grateful for. Or just write down words in your gratitude journal like, love, peace, clarity, fun, joy, bliss and so forth. There is a power in the written word; it seems to solidify your appreciative thoughts to a deeper level and it keeps more of the same coming our way.

It is true that gratitude brings abundance, prosperity, peace, and grace into your life. But an even more important reason to come to gratitude is that it just simply feels good, right now! Even a little bit of gratitude nourishes the soul and heals the body and mind.

If you want to be inspired to be in gratitude, read Pam Grout's book, *Thank & Grow Rich: A 30-Day Experiment in Shameless Gratitude and Unabashed Joy*. This book will make you smile, laugh out loud, and dance with gratitude! Pam Grout is the queen of gratitude.

Kindness

Despite what you might have been told, we're not inherently selfish. The truth is we're inherently kind.

−DAVID HAMILTON, PHD, AUTHOR

To be kind is a sure way to enhance your life in more ways than you might expect. First of all it makes us feel good to be kind, it brings fulfillment and joy to our lives, and it makes others feel good as well. Kindness is invaluable for the survival and evolution of the human species. Being kind to one another keeps us connected on all levels, emotional, physical, and spiritual. Working together especially during difficult times has helped preserve the species over thousands of years. Kindness in relationships creates a lasting bond and a desire to stay together—it creates true love. Science shows that when we are kind or we are receiving kindness or even if we are observing an act of kindness, our bodies and minds are boosted with wellness. Acts of kindness produce oxytocin, a hormone produced by the pituitary gland, which in turn produces nitric oxide, a substance produced by our bodies that prevents and even reverses cardiovascular disease. Nitric oxide keeps us young, it slows aging by reducing muscle degeneration and inflammation in the body, and helps to remove free radicals in the body, which cause aging. Being kind makes us happier, healthier, and has been scientifically proven to alleviate depression, high blood pressure, and social anxiety.

One of the best books I've read on kindness is that by David Hamilton, *The 5 Side Effects of Kindness*." You will feel so good after reading this book—it is full of the science behind the positive side effects of kindness. The five side effects of kindness that he discusses in his book are;

- **Kindness** Makes us Happier.

- **Kindness** Is Good for the Heart.

- **Kindness** Slows Ageing.

- **Kindness** Improves Relationships.

- **Kindness** is Contagious.

You can't go wrong with being kind, go for it!

The Power of Forgiveness

Forgiveness is the fragrance that the violet sheds on
the heel that has crushed it.

–MARK TWAIN, AUTHOR

Forgiveness is crucial to a healthy, happy, and productive life. And it doesn't matter if you were the victim or the perpetrator. Forgiveness sets your heart free from heaviness and unnecessary burdens that can weigh you down. Not forgiving someone does not give you power, rather it poisons you. It simply is not good for you or anyone around you. As one remains in anger and resentment, one attracts more of that energy to enter their life. Do you want anger and resentment or do you prefer peace, joy, and love in your life? I forgive because I want to live a life of joy and love and I consciously choose not to live with anger and resentment.

Not forgiving keeps you in the past and keeps you resistant to healing and moving forward. It is much easier to forgive when you realize that the past is done and cannot be different than it is. I do not want to be held hostage by the past. Can you see how living in acceptance and presence is crucial to our ability to forgive fully?

When you forgive someone, it does not mean you need to spend time with him or her or condone the deed that hurt you. What it means is that you are taking the situation to a higher place of release and non-judgment. A small price to pay for freedom. Their actions and their state of mind will continue to affect their life, but it does not have to continue to affect your life, unless you harbor and nurture their actions by feeding them daily with your attention through your thoughts and emotions. What good does that do? Those toxic states of mind are damaging to your health and well-being. This has been scientifically proven over and over. You can do what you need to do for your safety and to remedy the particular situation, but then let it go.

Sometimes what we most need to forgive is ourselves and our judgments. I try to see my part in any discord and to learn from the mistakes I have made. . I rather love my fellow human, see down to their soul, have empathy, and let go. I cannot control what they choose to do. Sometimes, it is the ones who committed the harsh actions that cannot do the forgiving. They feel that if they forgive and forget, it might make them wrong. They feel they have to stick to their story. It seems to be those steeped deep in fear, ego, and heavy identification with their story that have the hardest time forgiving.

When we begin to see life from present moment awareness, we realize that in reality nothing could diminish our true Essence. What I have come to learn as I look deeply into the act of forgiveness is that there really is no such thing as forgiveness. This may be hard to grasp at first, but stick with me here. Everyone is living at a different level of consciousness. Many are just not in a place where they can even conceive of forgiveness, others, cannot conceive of not forgiving. This realization is an important step out of recreating patterns of cause and effect in our lives. We are not creating more karma to deal with; we have come to a higher understanding of the laws of the universe and consciousness and we realize that hate and judgement are not real in our universe of connection and love. We rewire our mindset and recreate our world by letting go of holding someone responsible for our unhappiness and using the person as our reason to justify hatred. We realize because of the level of conscious evolution, they could not have done any better.

In this section, I am speaking again from direct experience. I have forgiven the men who murdered my brother. I have unfortunately had many other hard things to forgive, as so many of us do. I now have the deeper understanding as mentioned above, so it is actually incorrect to say "I have forgiven." It is not my place to judge, but I can understand the different levels of consciousness and hold myself accountable for my own state of consciousness.

An excellent book to learn tools to forgive and understand the importance of forgiveness would be Colin Tipping's, *Radical Forgiveness: Making Room for the Miracle*; it is a classic and the bible of forgiveness.

Self-Love

As a doctor, let me tell you what self-love does: It improves your hearing, your eyesight, lowers your blood pressure, increases pulmonary function, cardiac output, and helps wiring the musculature. So, if we had a rampant epidemic of self-love then our healthcare costs would go down dramatically. So, this isn't just some little frou-frou new age notion, oh love yourself honey. This is hardcore science.

–CHRISTIANE NORTHRUP, MD, AUTHOR

To love yourself and others is as essential to life as having air to breath. One of today's most influential teachers on self-love is Anita Moorjani, who had a profound near death experience (NDE), and wrote the book, *Dying to be Me.* Her most significant lesson from the other side was to love herself. Anita had severe cancer; her entire body was riddled with tumors and open sores. She was confined to a wheelchair and could not even hold up her head. In 2005, Anita went into a coma for thirty hours and everyone, including the medical staff, thought she would die. But to everyone's surprise she came out in a state of gratitude, love, and fearlessness. Within weeks the tumors dissipated and she became a medical miracle.

While experiencing her NDE she found that the underlying cause of her cancer was from her efforts to please everyone. She describes her past self as a "doormat," and a "people pleaser." Like most of us, and especially women, she was taught to put everyone else first and herself last.

Once she learned to love herself and to know her true Self, her health improved and she remains in good health today. Anita has dedicated her life to sharing her NDE and teaching others the invaluable lessons she learned on the other side. Self-love was the most important lesson of all. This is not to say if you have cancer or any other kind of illness you do not love yourself. Everyone's experience is different. The last thing one would want to do when they are sick is blame themselves. Every challenge in life has its own unique thread of realization for that individual. None of us consciously choose to hurt ourselves through our circumstances, but many children grow up feeling unworthy because of social conditioning and/or dysfunctional adults that are in charge.

When we talk about self-love, it is more than just loving our physical self and our personality, which, in actuality, is a very small part of our whole self. Our true Self, which is invisible, is much larger than our body, personality and thoughts. When we love ourselves, it is important to love our whole self, which includes the physical and the nonphysical. Our soul comes in with a purpose and if we do not love ourselves, we cannot even know what that purpose is. I feel everyone on earth has a primary purpose, which is to awaken to who we truly are. And the secondary purpose is your own individual passion that drives you to do the work that makes your heart sing, or as Sal would love to say, makes your boat float! If you spend all your time worrying about others and putting all your energy in making sure everyone around you is happy, you will not even hear the whispers of your soul speaking to you of your passion. Past trauma, fear, and living in the past can also muffle the quiet voice of the soul.

When we learn to love ourselves, it naturally leads to our awareness of who we truly are, and it allows us to thrive and enjoy life as we fulfill our purpose here on earth. When we begin to awaken, we realize that we are pure unconditional love, as is the Source of which we are all an extension of. To say, "love yourself," is actually incorrect. There is not two of you, the one who loves and the one who is you. There is only one, there is not you and yourself. The English language makes it sound like there is a you loving another self. No, it is just YOU, and YOU are pure love. When you feel this and realize the truth of this in every fiber of your being, then you are home.

Know Thyself

To know others is wisdom; to know thyself is enlightenment.

–*Lao Tzu, 601 BC, Author—Tao Te Ching*

When I use the ancient word "thyself" here and the way that Lao Tzu used it above, it means your formless true Self. There are many great tools presented here to overcome grief and transcend fear and negativity. These practices will lead to an awakened life, filled with love, gratitude, and peace. But the one thing that is needed for all of the other tools to work is to know thyself. To know thyself is not a tool, it is the goal of all the tools. In other words, without knowing who you truly are, beyond the body and thoughts, would be to live a life susceptible to fear. To live an unstable life that is not grounded or balanced would be a life of uncertainty and fragility. It would be like the wave of the ocean not realizing that it IS part of the entire ocean. The little wave is also made of H2O just like the deep, vast sea. When the wave sinks back into the sea, it does not cease to exist, but turns into another and another wave; it is always part of the sea and is never *not* part of the sea. Sometimes it can be seen as the wave, but other times it is deep at the bottom of the sea floor and cannot be seen at the surface. There is absolutely no separation of the wave and the vast sea. So it is with all of us—we are mostly formless, we *feel* our essence when we pay attention. It is not something to be described, rather it is to be *felt.*

The idea of enlightenment is usually thought to be granted to just a few individuals, and this has been true in the past of the fully enlightened humans on earth. However, awakening is a process for most and happens little by little. It's important to realize that the secret to enlightenment is that the seed of enlightenment is deep within each one of us and is always there ready to sprout. It has always been a part of every moment of our life. Whenever we notice the presence of our awareness, that thing inside of us that is observing us having an experience, we are realizing our Self, this is a touch of enlightenment in that moment. That Self recognition is the beginning of the awakening process and of true liberation.

One way that has helped me to feel my true essence, to know thyself, is by meditating on death. To meet the angel of death before death finds me; I know this sounds somewhat morbid, but it is not. When we find death, it opens us up to living life freely and fully, and releases our fear of death. It's a little bit like the classic play, *A Christmas Carol* by Charles Dickens, where Scrooge lives abundantly and passionately after he experiences his own death through his experience with the angel of death. You see this change in patients with cancer when they are given only a few months or a few years to live. Sometimes they change their way of being in the world in such a positive way that the cancer just dissipates.

Take some time to yourself and think deeply about life—what is constant in your life. Everything eventually dissolves in your life, including your body at death. When you realize that nothing is constant, if you go a little deeper on this thought, you realize there is a part of you that is constant. Can you feel that part of you that has always been there, when you think back as far as you possibly can, maybe when you were just a toddler and then you feel every other stage of your life from adolescence to each decade up to where you are now, can you feel that part of you that was always there no matter what age you were at or are? And if you think of when you die, what part of you will still be there, can you feel that same part of you that has always been there, cannot be taken with death? You can feel that your body and your personality with the story of the person you have been will be gone, but that subtle part of you remains. There are no words to describe this; it can however be felt. It feels like the one who is looking behind the eyes, listening, and experiencing, and the closest word to describe it might be Presence. Meditate on this and feel the freedom and joy it brings as you become aware of your true Essence and immortality.

This topic of knowing oneself, awakening, is interwoven throughout this book. I feel Self-realization, awakening, enlightenment (all synonyms) are the primary reason we are all here. Loss and trauma and suffering in general are what take most of us to awakening. But we do not need to suffer anymore to awaken. Practice the tools provided here that resonate with you and sharpen your awareness with meditation and present moment living and see what happens. Keep your intention strong to live a life of peace and harmony, stay in gratitude, and know that *love* is always the way. This life is but a blink of an eye in eternity, live it to your highest standard, treat each person as though they are a reflection of yourself (because they are), and learn and grow as much as you can.

Love turns man into an ocean of happiness, an image of peace,
a temple of wisdom. Love is every man's very Self, his true beauty,
and the glory of his human existence.

–Swami Muktananda

It is important to remember that enlightenment is not a goal, we all have everything we need and we know everything we need to know, we just need to remember and to realize this truth.

Summary of Part III

Reading all of these suggestions to ease from the ill effects of adversity into thriving may sound overwhelming but almost all of them are suggesting a mindset and a way of being in the world. Being present, living a surrendered life, enjoying humor, connection, and nature can accurately be called a lifestyle.

If you are not practicing any of these things at this time, just start with fifteen minutes of meditation every morning and see how it goes. You can see how you feel and add on from there. Take it in baby steps and keep it simple. When we take one small action at a time and we practice with consistency and perseverance, it inevitably leads to greatness. You may find that you are already doing some of these things, pick the ones that resonate with you and go from there. You can definitely do this.

CLOSING THOUGHTS

Life Continues and Loss Is Part of Life

Each man had only one genuine vocation - to find the way to himself....
His task was to discover his own destiny - and to live it out within himself.
Everything else was only a would-be existence, an attempt at evasion,
a flight back to the ideals of the masses, conformity and fear of one's
own inwardness.

–HERMAN HESSE, NOBEL PRIZE–WINNING AUTHOR

I have walked through fire these past seven years, not only from losing a child but also my best friend only two years after Sal's passing. I met Denise in first grade; we were both five years old, and we stayed best friends throughout the rest of life. We were never apart for more than three months during our entire lives. Since we were five years old, we have celebrated every birthday of our lives together. Not only did we go through grammar school and high school together, we went away to college together. After college we backpacked through Europe together. We lived together before we got married and were great roommates. She liked the yoke of the egg and I like the white, we were beyond compatible. We got proposed to on the same day and both of our children are exactly nine months apart, with zero planning. Each time I went to visit her in the hospital, after she had a baby, I was pregnant, but did not know it. She got the girls I wanted, and I the boys she wanted. As strange as it seems, we never really got in an argument. We just knew we both loved each other and that was never going to be in question. We witnessed each other's life from as far back as we could remember. We were always supportive of each other. Denise was a fun person to be around, her deep boisterous laugh was contagious as was her huge smile. I am eternally grateful that I had a friend like Denise. How many people are graced with a friend from first grade until the end of their days on earth? Denise was not spiritual the way I was, until Sal passed. Sal's passing opened her up and she became much more in tune with spirituality. She witnessed what happened to me, and since we were so connected, it transformed her too. She called me her hero after Sal passed. She knew all the signs that Sal had sent me and was amazed. She helped me with all the fundraisers I organized to build Sal's yurt. Denise was Italian and loved, more than anything, to cook for family and friends. She made most of the food for these fundraisers. We enjoyed making up the menu together. Her generosity lifted my spirits and touched me to the core of my being. After Sal passed, she would come over and bring food for my family; her food was infused with so much love, that whatever it was, tasted so good and was so healing to the soul! Even her thinly sliced salami was healing for me.

A few weeks before she passed, she told me she had a very vivid dream of Sal. She and Sal were close as she witness his life. They were very much alike in some ways. They both had big personalities and the capacity to be the life of the party. They were social and loved people. They both had tons of friends and everyone loved to be with them, because of their high vibration. In Denise's dream, Sal and Denise were cooking together. This was a favorite thing for Denise to do with Sal. She told me, Sal was happy and they were laughing together. She said he looked vibrant and they were having so much fun together. The dream was vivid and she remembered it well. Then she said, I feel like he was preparing me to make my transition. I laughed it off and said, you better not do that! But only six weeks later, she passed due to breast cancer. She fought with every fiber of her being to stay here on earth; she was beyond brave in my eyes, and she had become my hero—actually she always was. So many of us needed her bright light. Once again, I was forced to go into acceptance. This was so hard for me, since I had just lost Sal. It seemed surreal and so unfair. I have had more than my share of loved ones already on the other side. The only good thing about it is that when it is time for my transition, there is going to be a big party over there! But, all jokes aside, again it is a knowing that the divine order of the universe is something I trust, honor, and accept. Denise, like Sal, is with me and we are consistently developing our vibrational relationship.

Through all this loss, it became crystal clear to me what is truly real in this life. What is real is love, harmony, connection, and presence, this is all I want now. My relationships with those who truly love without an agenda have grown and deepened. My awareness has deepened and my clarity has grown, the egoic part of me, my small self was limiting me and causing drama, blinding me to my infinite potential as a human being. Realizing that what lies beneath the surface of my personality is a powerful consciousness that is pure unconditional love. And it connects everyone and everything in a oneness that cannot be explained, but can be felt in the depths of silence.

The Truth About "Death"

Each night, when I go to sleep, I die. And the next morning, when I wake up, I am reborn.

–Mahatma Gandhi

Death is our greatest adventure in life. Sal has made it clear to me that he is in a wonderful place, and as I wrote in Part II, I have felt the overpowering feeling of the unconditional love that is the natural state in this formless realm. In this place we are all accepted and loved unconditionally. So many of the near-death experiences talk about this and of the beautiful white light that emanates this deep love. Dr. Zach Bush. MD, has stated that almost every time he resuscitates a patient in the ICU, the first thing they say is, why did you bring me back? No matter what age, gender, nationality, or occupation.

Denise was terribly sick, yet fighting for her life so hard, but once again through Denise I got a glimmer of the afterlife. She took me with her as far as I could go without my body leaving earth. If she knew what was in store for her, she might have let go of her sick body sooner.

I had been commissioned to teach yoga for a week aboard a vacation sailboat during the time Denise was struggling with the cancer. The trip was in the Caribbean and I was taking my friend, Karen, who lived in Florida. Denise and her boyfriend, George, were going to come, as well as other friends and family members. With Denise's illness, she and George had to cancel months before. As this sailboat adventure was getting near, Denise was getting worse. I talked with her and told her I was going to cancel. She became upset and did not want me to cancel. During the time I was away on the trip, her conditioned worsened. When I returned to Karen's house in Florida, I called George to find out how she was doing, he told me the bad news. I was devastated and wanted to fly home immediately, but I could not change my flight, the website was completely down for the airline I was flying on. I could not do anything about my flight, but I was scheduled to leave in two days. George said he didn't think she was going to pass in the next few days, but that she was much worse. Of course, he was hopeful as we all were. Since I couldn't leave the next day, I told Karen, there was only one place I wanted to be in Florida. I wanted to go to Michael Singer's place to hear his usual weekly talk. Michael Singer is a favorite spiritual teacher of mine. We left immediately for the five-hour road trip, and got there just in time to join the satsang, (sacred gathering). The first thing out of his mouth was, "There really are no problems." It may sound strange, but I immediately knew this was the sentence I needed to hear at that moment. I completely felt the truth of this odd statement as my best friend was about to exit the earth. But what I realized is that death is really not a problem in the big picture of eternity, especially not for the person who is making their transition. It can be a big problem for those of us left behind; we can suffer deeply and in our humanness we do. But, if we step out of our smallness and into our grandness, we realize this is a part of life that is inevitable and it is our perception that makes it become a problem for us. When I've lost loved ones who are physically suffering, there is always a relief that they are free of pain and a knowing that they are now in their true home.

The next day I was packing up to leave and go home. As I was packing, I picked up my cell phone and called Denise's daughter, Nicole. Nicole answered and told me that her mom was not speaking, her eyes were open, and she was staring up at the ceiling. I asked Nicole to put her cell phone on speaker and to hold it up to her mother's ear. I began to guide my best friend to her real home. I told Denise, to not be afraid, it was okay to let go, she had fought hard, but now it was time to let go. I told her she would be safe and stay conscious throughout her transition, that Sal, her Dad, and other loved ones would be there to greet her. She would not be alone, she would feel the most incredible love she ever felt in her entire life. I told her I loved her so much and so did her family and so did many other people. I told her she was amazing and made everyone's life better who knew her and she would always be with her loved ones. Only her daughters and George were in the room as this was happening. Nicole told me later, that when I hung up, they lovingly repeated to Denise the things I had said.

I did the call and the guidance without any thought on my part at all. I was doing this almost on autopilot. If I had thought about it, I probably would not have done it, I might have been worried that her daughters would be upset that I was not encouraging her to fight for her life and I was encouraging her to pass. But that is not at all what happened. I was being guided by an Infinite Intelligence that guided my every move and my every word at this point. I simply surrendered to this higher power that was guiding me. What happened next was quite phenomenal...

After I made the call to Denise, Karen and I starting walking down the street from her home to catch a quick dinner. As we were walking I started feeling a huge sense of relief. I could literally feel myself being lifted upward, I felt light and free. Then I felt emotions of excitement and fun, it was a feeling of seeing those you love that you haven't seen in a long time. And then I felt so much happiness and joy. I looked at Karen and said my best friend is dying, why I am feeling so elated? This is so strange! Minutes later I got a text from Denise's sister, Darlene—it said Denise had passed. All of this happened only twenty minutes after I had gotten off the phone with Denise. When Karen and I walked back to her house, the sky had opened up with huge evening sunrays on puffy clouds and I looked at Karen and said, there's a big party going on in heaven right now. It was so strange, because again I felt devastated from the loss of Denise and my heart broke for her daughters, family, George, and myself. But I felt a sense of deep love and gratitude that Denise was in a wonderful place with her father who she loved so much and that she was not suffering anymore. She suffered long enough. I know that she is with me and her loved ones, I see her daughters as my own and I love to be with them whenever I can. They are both amazing young woman and so precious to me. I am grateful for our special bond that only grows deeper with time.

We easily see the beauty in birth, but most of us fail to see the beauty in death. If we can think of death as a form of birth, it would lead us closer to the truth about death. Death is a transformation from our limited physicality to our free natural Being in the formless realm. Death is a liberation—be prepared for this liberation by dying before you die through contemplation and meditation. And through living life fully without reservation and without fear. See death for what it truly is—a transition of complete freedom. Like the caterpillar waking up as the ethereal butterfly.

There is a Life Force in All Living Things That Want to Thrive

When you arise in the morning think of what a privilege it is to be alive, to think, to enjoy, to love….

–Marcus Aurelius, second-century Roman Emperor

When I think of examples of life wanting to thrive, I look at how true this is in nature. We've seen plants in an arid area growing out of rocks. In my garden, wildflowers grow out of the pavers. They seem to grow out of nowhere, with no water or light, yet they make their way to the surface from the darkness below. There is the kangaroo rat that lives in the dessert in North America and drinks no water, it has adapted to survive from getting enough moisture from the seed diet.

Many of us are devastated after losing the person who is so dear to us that we just lose our drive to live, let alone thrive. We must take one day at a time, sometimes even one breath at a time. We have a natural life force in us that wants to thrive. We are meant to live life to the fullest. Our spirit loved ones want us to still play with them and more than anything they want us to realize we have everything we need already to live a full life. If you are the one left behind, take it as a clear sign that you are the one who is meant to expand, thrive, and awaken here on earth.

We are meant to live in the present. Life here on earth goes on for us. We are meant to meet new people and to continue to engage with our loved ones here on earth. We are not meant to live in the past and mourn endlessly. You might have tried that and so you know it feels awful and you intuitively know that it is not the path of your evolution. You can feel in the depths of your being that your primal urge is to survive and thrive. Just like the plants that thrive with no light or water, they find a way and so do we. To be genuinely cheerful in the face of adversity is a sign of spiritual development. Hence, the quote below from the Self-Realized Master, Paramahansa Yogananda:

If you can hold onto your happiness during all the difficulties in your life, then you will begin to rise above the influence of the stars. If you can retain your smile in spite of repeated challenges, that is a sign of the awakening of the consciousness of divinity within you. Through all such actions, you are changing your body and mind and how they are affecting the twelve centers in your spine. As a result of these changes, the stars will begin to smile upon you.

Yogananda is not taking about smiling while your heart is breaking here. No, he is talking about being able to understand the larger picture of life, the divine order of the universe, and trusting in a higher power. He's talking about being able to live with true joy and an inner knowing of the true essential nature of the Self. All of this has been repeatedly spoken of throughout this book. He is not being poetic, when he speaks of the twelve energy centers along the spine, he is speaking of our chakras (energy centers) and our neurology. When you live this way, your neurology is rewired and you literally change your physiology and your mindset. This is shown today through science, and yet the great sages spoke of this long ago. Just like the Kangaroo rat and plants evolved in order to thrive without water, our neurology has also figured out how to thrive after a deep loss.

Dr. Joe Dispenza and other science-based, spiritual teachers are demonstrating this in their workshops where people have been spontaneously healing from years of chronic diseases after one week of monitored intense meditation.

You are powerful enough to influence matter because at
the most elementary level, you are energy with a consciousness.
You are mindful matter.

–Dr. Joe Dispenza, Author, Scientist

Take your loved one with you as the twinkle in your eyes, and begin to thrive even more than you ever have before, knowing that you actually have an invisible companion that has your back from the formless realm.

I have learned that we can and will be together forever with our loves ones if we so choose. Bonds of unconditional love and heaven are states of consciousness, not necessarily places we go to only when we die. I choose to dwell in those states of consciousness as much as possible. May we all realize that we are here to expand our consciousness and come to the realization that we are all droplets of the Infinite Spirit, we are One with our Source and with each other. If this rings true, how could we not be together forever with each other and with our Source. We are never apart, never alone; hence we are **together forever** with God and our loved ones. This is the amazing blessing of loss on this earth school. Awaken to the truth and live only with your birthright of love, connection, and peace. Another blessing in disguise of loss and pain here on earth is that our empathy and compassion for others grows and our hearts soften for our fellow human travelers of this earth school. And then we also begin to have compassion for ourselves as well.

This illusory earth world is needed for Source to be realized. It is through the world and ultimately through us that the Unmanifested knows itself. When we realized this, we live a purposefully life that is rich in ever new consciousness. Let the veil between form and formlessness thin out and allow the adventurous life you were meant to live unfold. After all, it's all in divine order. Trust and let go.

Thank you for reading my story. My greatest wish is that it has eased you or prevented you from prolonged grief, enhanced your connection with your loved ones, knowing that even though they are no longer on earth, your strong bond of deep love is in no way diminished.

I will end with a poem I wrote for Sal and gave to him on Christmas Eve. Sal had just turned seven however, I still feel the same way about him to this day, his essence has never changed.

To Sal

The Sunshine of My Life

Wherever Sal stands the sun shines bright

He has bright sparkling blue eyes

He has a happy enlightened smile that melts my heart every time!

He has the voice of an angel and the heart of Santa Claus

He's my special seven year old that lights up my world!

Merry Christmas

Love You Always and Forever,

Mommy

ACKNOWLEDGEMENTS

I am eternally grateful for all of my family, friends, and students who have been exceptionally supportive through the losses I have encountered in just a few years, the loss of my son, Sal, best friend, Denise and divorce from a marriage of 32 years. Without their love, encouragement, and friendships, I'm not sure that I would have been able to transcendent these losses into growth and deep inner peace. Many of them have encouraged me to write this book, and even strangers I have met along the way have encouraged me to tell my story so that it may help others.

I want to thank my dedicated students, who have witness my journey first hand and have encouraged me to offer what I have learned and what I have shared with them. I am grateful to Geri Jones, Lauren Ward, Sally Servidio, Arthur O'Brien, Kelsey Guntren, and Dustin Berkowitz for contributing their experiences with Sal in Part 11 of Together Forever. I'd like to thank Nancy Vierra my editor and dear friend. I'd like to thank Gail LaMar, Karen Satterlee, Linda Thorlakson, Hilary Nouri, Melinda Dunn, Pam Grout, Dr. Vijay Jain, and Gurudev for taking the time to read Together Forever, before it was published and have offered me feedback and encouragement to publish my book. I also would like to thank Patrick Aylward of bookbaby for his help throughout the publishing process. A special thank you to my friend, Ken Hettman who made life easier for me so I was able to put the hours in to make this book a possibility. I'd like to thank Nick Ramirez, who would meet me for coffee at any hour of the day and reminded me to laugh through all the hard times.

And a giant thank you to my son, Arthur, who stood by me always and never waived his integrity to take the easy way out. His love, hugs, and dedication keep me grounded and optimistic. And lastly, a big shout out of gratitude to my son Sal, whose constant inspiration and subtle whispers wrote this book with me. Sal is always here for me and his intense love continues to carry me through life on a magical joy filled wave. Finally, I would like to express my gratitude to our One Source for the inspiration, synchronicities, and beauty that gave this book Life.

ABOUT THE AUTHOR

Anna Marie Enea recently moved to the lush forest in Oregon to be with her son, Arthur. She was born, raised, and lived most of her in life in Northern California, except the year she lived on the island of Maui and worked for the state as a public health educator. She holds a Master's in exercise physiology and nutrition, a Bachelor of Science in health science/public health, and an RDH (registered dental hygienist). She has advanced certifications for teaching yoga and meditation from both Amrit Yoga Institute in Florida and Ananda's Expanding Light in Northern California. She has taught yoga, yoga nidra, meditation, spirituality, nutrition, exercise, wellness, forest bathing, and hiking for the past 40 years. She loves to share her joy of travel by leading retreats to Italy, Hawaii, California, and Oregon.

Website for Together Forever and updates on retreats and classes: choosetotalwellness.org.

Sal Enea O'Brien